THE ROAD
to
NEW LIFE

THE ROAD
to
NEW LIFE

◆ THE WAY OF JESUS OF NAZARETH ◆

PHIL REHBERG

DISCIPLE
PUBLISHING

ISBN 13: **9780692310632**.
ISBN 10: **0692310630**.
Library of Congress Catalog Card Number: 2009910159

CONTENTS

INTRODUCTION

IF YOU ARE open to God, this book is for you. It is about God reaching out to you and inviting you into an eternal friendship.

Take time to consider each section in the chapters and let God's message of salvation capture your heart. Remember to consider the reflection questions and prayers at the end of each section. They will help lead you to a new life.

Quotations from the Bible are from the New American Standard Bible, unless letters in parentheses after the quotations or in the footnotes indicate other versions. The letters NLT stand for the New Living Translation, and the letters NIV stand for the New International Version, both of which are popular contemporary versions of the Bible.

CHAPTER 1

LOVE, SIN, AND SEPARATION

The Story of Love and the Beginning of Sin

SINCE BEFORE TIME and space, God has existed in a perfect community of love. The three—God the Father, God the Son, and God the Holy Spirit—are one divine Being[1] and take great joy in their relationship. God is a mysterious unity of three persons in one Being, a tri-unity,

---

[1] See Matthew 28:19.

the Trinity. The three live, create, and act together in one perfect harmony.

This one Trinity experiences indescribable happiness every moment of his being. God is beautiful beyond description. He *is* truth, and this brings him constant peace and satisfaction. Nothing false dwells within him to cloud his judgment. He is goodness without corruption. All his thoughts and actions are pure and free from selfishness. The three persons of the Trinity continuously give and joyously receive from each other.

> *They enjoyed constant happiness and satisfaction with God and with one another.*

God is also endlessly powerful and creative, and he took great joy in creating a universe to display his love and power. He took even greater joy in creating man and woman, beautiful beings who reflected his great qualities.[2] He created them for a community of love with him. All the things he created were in perfect harmony with their Creator, and they enjoyed constant happiness and satisfaction with God and with one another.

The man and woman enjoyed the thrill of perfect, selfless love for each other. Their community of love was a reflection of the community of love enjoyed by the Trinity. Every day they found new adventures with God and discovered more about him and his creation.

God created man and woman with the highest purpose of all: to receive and give love.[3] He considered them his children and loved them with an infinite, all-powerful love beyond anything they could imagine. In return they loved him from the depths of their hearts. He desired them, and

---

[2] Genesis 1:26.

[3] Matthew 22:36–40

2

they desired him, and he delighted in this communion with his creation.

But God also gave this man and woman freedom to choose against him, because in order for love to be genuine, it must have the freedom to choose. Some angels had already chosen against him, and they became spirits of darkness. These fallen angels (demons) were determined to ruin God's creation and destroy the humans.

Satan, the leader of the dark spirits, tempted the humans to disobey God and become like him. The first man and woman were attracted to this prideful idea and took the bait.[4] Sadly, all humans who have come after them are infected by their sin and repeat it.[5]

> *They chose against him. This broke his heart and broke their relationship with him and with each other.*

This is the great tragedy of human history. When God gave the man and woman the choice of living by their own knowledge of good and evil or living by the life that comes from the Creator, they chose against him. This broke his heart and broke their relationship with him and with each other.[6] It destroyed the community of love. They chose not to be his children. This is the definition of sin: the destruction of relationship. Sin is breaking the law of love.[7]

All humans inherited this brokenness from the man and woman so we too could no longer live in God's kingdom, in his perfect world of love. We were separated from the

---

[4] See Genesis 3.

[5] Romans 5:12; 1 Corinthians 15:22.

[6] Romans 2:20–25.

[7] In Romans 2:2–28, we see how humans decided against a loving, worshipping relationship with God and how that sin brought God's judgment on them.

source of love and goodness. Thus, we lost our ability to love with pure hearts.[8]

We now have a huge relationship hole deep in our hearts where God used to be. Whether we feel it or not, our spirits are lonely for God, and nothing else can satisfy that longing. We try to fill the hole with friends, money, success, knowledge, or pleasure, but nothing brings deep satisfaction. We are in deep need of God, but our hearts are twisted, so we turn to other things instead of to him.

In the process of seeking satisfaction,[9] we invent ways to destroy relationships, in other words, to sin. We rebel against God by constantly breaking his law of love. We lust to take from others instead of giving in love. We tell lies to get what we want, even though those lies wreck relationships. We disconnect sex from the eternal bond it should create. We look for ways to control others for our own benefit. We give our affection to wealth instead of to God and others. We hurt others out of our own fear, pain, and insecurity.

We feel shame for the things we do and for the things others do to us. We reject others, and we reject ourselves. We are in a prison of guilt, shame, and lost relationships.

Sometimes we are happy, but other times we are empty. Sometimes we love, and sometimes we hate. Sometimes we create, and sometimes we destroy. And we know things are not as they should be.

Our minds are dark because we are disconnected from the source of truth. We call our wrongdoings "mistakes." We blame people who hurt us for the way we act.[10] And we believe untruths about ourselves and about the Creator that

---

[8] See Romans 2:24–29.

[9] See Romans 1:28–32.

[10] Abusive environments can cripple our ability to love others. Yet this is not an excuse for hurting others.

4

prevent us from finding peace and happiness. We imagine that we are gods of our own lives, or we create imaginary gods to worship. We rebel against the true Creator and rob him of his glory by not giving him credit for his creation.[11] He still loves us and gives us good things, but we find many reasons to avoid following him.

Thus, we have lost the ability to live in a community of love. This is what we call "the fall." Our human natures and all of nature itself fell into a corrupted state. When we chose against God, our very natures changed so that we became unable to reflect him as we were meant to. In other words, we were no longer good by nature. Sin polluted our inner-most beings like a poisonous spill that kills

> *We are like a river that looks healthy on the surface but is mostly dead.*

the life of a river. So we are like a river that looks healthy on the surface but is mostly dead underneath. Now we actually oppose God by nature. When we disconnected from him, we lost our peace, we lost our freedom, we lost our happiness, we lost our selflessness, we lost our purpose, we lost our meaning, and we lost perfect love.

We left God's family. We are no longer his children, and he is no longer our Father. He is our Father in the broad sense that he is our Creator but not in the sense of our everyday relationship with him.

We still have consciences that tell us right and wrong, but we can no longer perfectly choose good because our natures are damaged by separation from our Creator. We do some good things, but his image in us is shattered. Now we are broken reflections of his glorious nature. Some part of

---

[11] Romans 1:20–22.

5

us knows this, but more often we pretend that everything is okay.

We conveniently forget how far from godliness we really are. We learn how to dull our consciences. Many of us even convince ourselves that we are not sinners—that we do not break the law of love in our daily lives.

Some of us made up our own religions or philosophies to get back to God, to feel better about ourselves, or to justify our own broken ways, but none of this brings happiness. We could never recover the joy, truth, and beauty that God originally gave us.

Yet the Creator still desires us. He longs for us and wants a friendship with us. He cares about our thoughts and feelings. He values us more than we can know. So he did not give up on us after the fall. He spoke through people to explain what had happened to us. He also gave us the Ten Commandments and other commandments to follow so we would learn how to live in communities of love. This is referred to as the Law.

But even the few who tried to follow the Law could not do it very well.

For reflection and prayer

Do you ever feel something missing deep in your heart? Can you describe it?

Ask God to show you what is missing.

Do you have ways of trying to fill what is missing? Have they satisfied you?

Do you think of God as wanting to be close to you and to bless you?

Are you open to letting God fill what is missing in your heart?

Conviction: The Gift of Recognizing Our Sins

The Creator wants to make us his children again. He gave us an invitation to come back to him. This invitation or message is referred to as the *gospel*, which literally means "good news." The gospel is God's plan for our salvation and is explained in chapter 2.

But when we chose against him, our hearts permanently lost their perfect love and their bond with God. So he must change our hearts. But first we must recognize that something is wrong with our hearts. Because of his love, he wants to show us this truth about ourselves so we can be reunited with him.

> *We have broken the community of love with God and with others.*

Thus, we need to be convicted of this truth. Conviction is a key element of the gospel. It is recognizing that we are sinners—that we have broken the community of love with God and with others. It is a great gift to be convinced of this truth, that we are not who we should be and that we really do commit sins. Sin separates us from our life, our source—from our Creator and Father. Seeing this truth is the first step toward freedom.

Even if we don't believe we are sinners, it should be clear that we are. We indulge in selfishness. We violate our consciences just for our own benefit. We steal. We lie. We shade the truth. We control others. We create unjust governments. We kill people in our hearts. We lust and imagine sleeping with other men's wives. We gossip. We obsess about our appearances and neglect what's inside. We get addicted. We buy things to make us feel better. We hurt others unintentionally because of our carelessness or ignorance. We divorce and rob our children of living with

7

both of their parents. We destroy the environment for selfish reasons. We hide from our own guilt and shame.

Even if we don't do these things, which is unlikely, we are still guilty of breaking God's law of loving others with pure hearts. And we are all guilty of ungratefulness and rebellion until we come to God. We are guilty for not showing gratitude to him for the good things we have and for all the good things on earth. It is a slap in God's face to withhold the honor and worship due him. We rebel by taking charge of our own lives, which is mutiny against the Lord of all. He created us to be his children, but we left him and imagine we can make a life without him.

Some of us are so damaged by our parents or others who hurt us that it is hard to see past our pain and realize that we are sinners. We only feel the sins others have committed against us. God knows our pain and even shares in it. He is sad that we suffer. He has special compassion for those who have been hurt or abused by others.

But he is the one who can heal and give true life. Our own weakness and sinfulness keep us from healing. When we are hurt, we respond in an unloving way, which is our sinfulness taking control. We hold anger and unforgiveness in our hearts, we take out our pain on others, and we even blame God and stay away from him. If we are willing to see the crookedness and lack of love in our hearts, then we will realize that we are sinful, and we can begin our journey back to God.

We may try to live good lives and think God will accept us because of our efforts. Even though God still deeply loves us, we cannot reach him by our own goodness. God wants us to follow our consciences and do good things, but this does not erase the sinfulness inside us and reunite us with God. If we are honest, we will realize that impurity and separation from God dwell deep inside us. We fall short of what we should be.[12]

Even if we do not commit obvious sins, no one is truly good. We may think we are good, but that is only because we don't know true goodness. True goodness is patience that doesn't end. Complete forgiveness without anger when we are wronged. Always loving. Always truthful. Never selfish. Never concerned about our egos. Never lustful. Never grabbing power for our own benefit. Never controlling. Never defensive when criticized. Never in fear because we trust God perfectly at all times. No one is this good.

So the first step back to God is allowing him to convict you about your sins. You can ask him to convict your heart. And when you feel conviction coming, don't block it, but let it do its work. Your denial only keeps you from finding true life. Honesty is the doorway back to his life and love for you. Let conviction wash over you and wake you up like a cold shower.

You know you are convicted of your sins when your soul is shaken and disturbed by your sins. You not only feel sorrow or remorse for your sins, but you also sense that you are out of relationship with God and others and need help.

> *Let conviction wash over you and wake you up like a cold shower.*

True conviction also brings dread because you know that justice requires that you pay the consequences for your sins—a never-ending separation from the source of life.

For reflection and prayer

Do you fail to love God and others as you should?
Do you feel convicted about your sins?

---

[12] Romans 3:23.

Prayer

Prayer asking God to give conviction of sin

God, I want to know you. Please show me my sins. I give you permission to reveal them to me. Show me how I break your law of love in many areas of my life. Show me how I do not love you and how I do not love others. And please convict me about how serious my sins are. I will let my heart feel the pain of knowing my sins. Let me have sorrow and remorse for them and help me see that my sins separate me from you. Give me the desire to seek salvation from my sins.

Separation from God

Because of our sins, we are and will be eternally separated from the union of love with God we were created for. Jesus and his apostles repeated this truth over and over in the New Testament.[13] Our sins separate us from God. Even though he wants friendship with us, our actions, our wills, and our natures all separate us from him. And because he is perfectly pure, he will not spend eternity with us as we are.

If our sins did not separate us from God, then there would be little need for Christ's coming and his message of salvation (in other words, the "gospel"). If we do not believe that our sins separate us from God, then we can only be "partial-born" Christians, never truly converted or transformed. Sadly, this problem is common today. Therefore, when we hear the gospel, we should open our hearts and let the Holy Spirit convict us of our sins and

---

[13] See Matthew 3:10–12; 13:40–42, 49–50; 25:41–46; Mark 16:16; Luke 16:19–31; John 5:28–29; 1 Corinthians 6:9–10; Galatians 5:19–21; Ephesians 5:5–6; 2 Thessalonians 1:7–9; 2:8–10; Hebrews 6:8; James 5:20; 2 Peter 2:9–17; Revelation 20:10–15; 21:8.

separation from God. Until that happens, we cannot walk the path of salvation through Jesus.

God cannot just overlook our sins. Should he overlook the sins of mass murderers or serial rapists? Why should he overlook our sins, even though they do not seem as serious? Does not justice require us to pay the consequences for our actions? Even if one we loved murdered someone, shouldn't he or she suffer the consequences? Likewise, God loves us, but he is also just and requires that justice be done.

So in order to rescue us from our sins, God has to cleanse us of our sins and change our hearts. But God will not force us to change against our wills. If your child grew up and decided that she did not want to have any relationship with you, would you try to force her to change her will? You may try to persuade her, but the decision is up to her. You can't force love; it has to be chosen freely.

We are like that child. God will not force us to change and come to him. He wants us to love him, and love requires freedom of choice. So we need to choose him freely. If we decide not to accept his offer of salvation, he will honor our decision and let us live apart from him forever.

We cannot be with him unless we recognize our sins and ask him to change us. Remember, a big barrier stands between us and God; our natures are not compatible with his. He is pure love, and our natures are corrupted with selfishness. The two cannot become one; they are like oil and water. He is pure; we are corrupt. He is honest; we deceive. He is coura- geous; we are fearful. He is forgiving; we are angry

> *The two cannot become one; they are like oil and water.*

and resentful. God won't make himself one with impure people, and we cannot change ourselves so we can be with him.

11

That is why humans could no longer live in his kingdom—paradise—after they chose sin. His kingdom is an extension of his perfect nature; it is not compatible with our corrupt natures. So the bad news is that our fate is to spend life on earth and eternity outside his kingdom unless he intervenes.

This eternal separation from his kingdom, presence, and love is called hell. We cannot even imagine how painful and unhappy that will be. Even the worst sinner on earth enjoys some of God's goodness and love here. All of us receive kindness from others. We all benefit from nature around us. We all experience some pleasure, whether from food or humor or sex or music or friends.

But in hell we will have none of these things. God's presence and the good things that come from him will be gone. We will have no pleasure, no friends, no love, no beauty, no songs, no laughter, no happiness, and no hope. Only pain, loneliness, suffering, and hatred. And we will never escape.

Thank God there is hope. Thank God that he sends people with the gospel of salvation to warn us of this. Thank God he convicts us of our sins. Thank God that we are heartbroken for what we have done. And thank God that he strikes us with the fear of eternity separated from him. This opens the door for God's amazing rescue.

For reflection and prayer

Do you think you are good enough to earn your way to being with God forever?

What would it be like to spend eternity away from all the good things on earth?

Ask God to show you the consequences of your sins.

Consider the prayer below. Pray it if it reflects your heart. (Do the same with prayers in other sections.)

Prayer

Prayer confessing that you are convicted you are a sinner

God, I realize you created me to love you and love others. I confess that I do not do this as I should. I have dishonored you by not letting you be Lord of my life. I have been selfish in my relationships with others, and I have hurt others. I know I have pride, anger, and unbelief. I try to satisfy myself with other pleasures instead of with you. I confess the other sins you have convicted me of: (Tell God all the sins you are aware of.) I know I am separated from you, and I need you to rescue me. Please lead me to salvation.

CHAPTER 2

THE STORY OF GOD SAVING HIS PEOPLE

God's First Agreement with His People

AFTER THE FALL, humans became increasingly evil. It looked like God would have to judge humans, and his great experiment would fail. But this is where the plot takes an astonishing twist.

Because of his great love, God devised a rescue plan. In about 2000 BC, he chose a man named Abraham, who lived in what is present-day Iraq.[1] He asked Abraham to leave homeland and relatives and to follow him to a new land. In return God would do several things:

1. He would give him many descendants and make him the father of a great nation.
2. He would give his descendants the land of Palestine for their home.
3. He would be his God and the God of his descendants.
4. He would bless all nations through him.

If Abraham were willing to leave his home, God would stay with him and his descendants and give them these great blessings. So God not only devised a plan to reunite with humans but also actually decided to bless them far beyond what they should have expected. He did not do this because Abraham earned it but as a gift. In spite of all the human sin, God would bless Abraham's descendants and the entire world through them. God would take a small tribe of nomads from the Middle East and bring salvation, cleansing of sin, and reunion with him to the whole world.

This is the plot of the entire Old Testament of the Bible. Would God's promises to Abraham be fulfilled?

Obstacles constantly arose. Abraham himself didn't always do the right thing, but he did trust God's words, and God considered him righteous for that.

Years passed until Abraham and his wife, Sarah, were over ninety years old, and they still did not have any children to fulfill God's promise. But God finally allowed them to conceive in their old age.

---

[1] The story of Abraham begins in Genesis 11:26.

Abraham's tribe slowly grew in Palestine. After three generations, a famine forced them to move to Egypt. Eventually, they became slaves for over four hundred years. God's plan for salvation seemed to be in danger; his chosen tribe, the Israelites, were slaves in a foreign land.

Then in about 1500 BC, God raised up Moses to lead the tribe.[2] God brought plagues on Egypt until the leader of Egypt, the Pharaoh, agreed to let them go. As they were leaving, Pharaoh changed his mind and sent his armies, perhaps the best in the world, to chase down the Israelites and pin them against the Red Sea. Again it looked like God's plan of salvation was doomed. But God parted the Red Sea, and when Pharaoh's armies tried to follow the Israelites through the sea, God sent the water crashing back over their heads to drown them.

Then God gave Moses commandments for living virtuous lives. This was called the Law. The most important commandments were about loving one another, respecting one another, sexual purity, helping strangers, helping the needy, and staying away from the false and unholy gods of neighboring tribes. He wanted

> *All the commands can be summed up in two commands: love God and love others.*

his people to be marked by humility, honesty, justice, mercy, and holiness. And love was at the center of the commandments. Jesus later explained that all the commandments can be summed up in two commands: love God and love others.[3]

God also set up a system of animal sacrifices so the people could be cleansed from their sins. Sin, the breaking of the law of love, was so serious that God required animals

---

[2] The story of Moses begins in Exodus 2.
[3] Matthew 22:37–40.

to die to pay for sin.[4] He allowed people to make sacrifices so they would not have to suffer for their own sins.

The agreements and commandments Yahweh (the name God gave himself, which is related to the phrase "I am") gave to Abraham and Moses are the old agreement or the old covenant. The Old Testament is the story of how this agreement played out in God's chosen people.

After Yahweh gave Moses the Law, he brought the Israelites back to Palestine where he helped them defeat many of the tribes living there. But the very next generation turned away from Yahweh. They mistreated each other, satisfied their own lusts, and stopped following Yahweh's commandments of love. So he stopped protecting them. He allowed one of the neighboring tribes to conquer the Israelites so that they would turn back to him, which they did. But soon the Israelites turned away from Yahweh again. God let another tribe conquer them again, and the whole cycle started over.

God's promises to Abraham and his commandments to Moses did not seem to be working. The chosen people did not have hearts for Yahweh, so they did not have the true life God wanted for them.

After about five hundred years of this, a man named David, who followed Yahweh with his whole heart, became king of the Israelites. God loved David and made an agreement with him that his kingdom would last forever. God was not giving up on his people.

But most of the kings who descended from David did not follow Yahweh, nor did the people. God sent prophets to warn them, but they did not listen. The prophets prophesied that a Messiah would come and save the people.

---

[4] Hebrews 9:22.

In 720 BC, Yahweh sent Assyria to conquer most of the Israelites; Assyria took them away, and the tribes lost their identities forever. In 586 BC, God sent Babylon to conquer the ones who remained—the Judahites or Jews. Many of the Jews were taken to Babylon.

At this point, everything looked bad for God's promises. The chosen people didn't follow God. Many who remained were captives in Babylon, not the Promised Land. They weren't blessing the world, and they didn't have a kingdom. Sin kept separating them from Yahweh.

But God sent the empire of Persia to free the Jews, and most returned to Palestine. Eventually, Greece conquered Palestine and the Jews. Later, the Romans conquered them. The promises to Abraham and of David's kingdom seemed a distant dream.

For reflection and prayer

God did not give up on his people in spite of their sins. Would he give up on you?

The Cross and the New Covenant

One day, during the time that the Romans ruled Palestine, God sent an angel to a Jewish woman named Mary.[5] The angel told her that God's Spirit would conceive a son inside her. He would be the Son of God and would inherit David's throne. Although he was God, he was born a little child in the town of Bethlehem.

When he had grown, Jesus declared that the kingdom of God was at hand. He taught about love, forgiveness, and humility and did great miracles by healing many people.

---

[5] This story is found in Luke 1:26–38.

He never wronged anyone; he always acted with love and justice, and he had a great heart for the needy and oppressed. No one before him ever did the things he did.

Jesus taught people that God was their Father and wanted to bless them. God would bless the poor and those who mourn, the gentle and the merciful, and those who hunger for what is right.[6] He taught them to love others the way they wanted to be loved. They should give to others, even if it means sacrifice. Amazingly, he said they should love their enemies.

Jesus promised peace and joy to those who followed him. His followers may not have wealth or popularity in this world, but they would have great rewards in the next life. And they could enjoy his kingdom community of love with his other followers now.

> *He taught them to love others the way they wanted to be loved.*

Jesus' teachings were so astonishing that people said no one had ever taught like him before. Many hoped that he was the promised Messiah who would lead them to victory over the Romans and establish a great Jewish kingdom.

So many people followed Jesus that the Jewish religious leaders became jealous and constantly opposed him. Most of them liked money, status, and making a show of their faith. Jesus reprimanded them and taught about the need for pure hearts.

The religious leaders finally talked one of Jesus' disciples into betraying him, and after a phony trial, they convinced the Roman leaders to crucify Jesus like a criminal. He died a painful death, hanging on a wooden cross. His disciples

---

[6] See Matthew 5 and Luke 6:20–38.

scattered. There was no Messiah, and the kingdom was dead.

Then came the plot twist to end all plot twists.

When some of his followers went to his tomb on the third day after his crucifixion, they found that his body was gone. He had risen from the dead! He appeared to hundreds of his followers and then ascended into heaven.

At last, his followers understood the Old Testament promises that predicted the coming of a Messiah who would die for his people.[7] Incredibly, Yahweh sent his Son to die for the sins of the people. Jesus never sinned, so he was the perfect sacrifice for human sin. The problem of sin was solved. Not only had Jesus taken the punishment for his people's sins,[8] but he also defeated the power of sin over their lives. No matter how much someone has sinned, Jesus offers forgiveness through the cross.

Jesus' resurrection also defeated the power of death so that all who choose to follow him are guaranteed a resurrection to new life. They do not need to fear death anymore. Instead, they can look forward to eternity the way it was meant to be.

After Jesus ascended into heaven, he sent the Spirit of God to indwell believers so they could overcome sin in their lives. The Holy Spirit actually gave birth to new natures inside believers that were loving and pure. Now believers could live Christlike lives. This is the new agreement or new covenant: whoever believes in the Son will have new life. The books of the New Testament are all about this new agreement.

Jesus' followers understood that the sacrificial system God established through Moses was only a temporary arrangement. It was a shadow of the perfect sacrifice to

---

[7] For example, see Isaiah 53.

[8] 1 Peter 2:24.

come when God the Son would offer himself as a sacrifice for sin. Now there were no more commandments to follow in order to receive forgiveness of sins. Our good works could never earn forgiveness of sins and reunion with God. Jesus did all the work and took the punishment for our sins through his death. Then God credited Jesus' sinless life to our account! We don't have to earn our way to God; he offers it as a gift. And by Jesus' resurrection, he defeated death and offers us new life. Now anyone who believes and surrenders to Jesus can have new life. This is the incredible good news. It is the best news any of us will ever hear.

So the commandments Yahweh gave the Israelites through Moses convicted people of their sins. The people learned that they could not follow the commandments and be good reflections of God's love. Their sin natures were too powerful. But in the new covenant, Jesus Christ defeated sin. Finally, God's followers could live godly lives from new hearts. They could find the abundant life God intended for his people. They were free from the spiritual power sin had over them.

The promises to Abraham and David were now being fulfilled through Jesus. God was bringing people all over the world back to himself. And his kingdom of love, peace, and justice had finally come through Jesus the King. This kingdom is constantly expanding through his followers, but it is not like an earthly kingdom or nation. One day it will come to fulfillment and will replace all earthly nations and all the suffering and sinfulness in the world.

For reflection and prayer

Are you attracted to Jesus' life and teachings? Why or why not?

Consider reading the book of Luke in the New Testament of the Bible. It tells the story of Jesus' life and teachings.

What Will You Do with the Cross?

This is the most astounding story in history. God himself became a mere man and allowed himself to be crucified like a criminal to bring us back to himself. The Son of God suffered so we could have life. This seems too incredibly good to be true. Yet this is the core of the gospel and the central truth of Christianity.

Christianity does not offer a Savior who beat the world at its own game. Jesus had no political power, no military power, no wealth, no academic degrees, and no earthly title. He never married, and he never enjoyed the "good life." Religious leaders rejected him, and his disciples abandoned him at the cross. He brought a kingdom that cannot be seen[9] and is not respected by worldly leaders. It is a kingdom of kindness, humility, and sacrificial love. Most of his followers were poor and uneducated.

He does not promise worldly success to those who follow him. He does not promise status or influence or respect. He does not promise wealth or comfortable lives. He does not promise to make us great intellectuals or great philosophers. But he does offer peace, satisfaction, truth, security, meaning, joy, and abundant life from deep inside. And he offers a community of love for all eternity.

Jesus invites everyone to follow him. He invites the worst of sinners. He invites the broken, the lost, the needy, the lonely, the abused, and the rejected. He invites the successful and wealthy who feel something missing. He invites anyone who wants to find God and the new life he gives.

---

[9] See Luke 17:20–21.

Will we accept Jesus' invitation to become his followers? Will we embrace the cross and Jesus' offer to forgive our sins and give us new life with God, or will we reject it? This is the challenge of the gospel.

The cross convicts us of our sins. Like a sword, it slices open our hearts and reveals the truth. The truth is that our sins, our failure to love, put Jesus on the cross. We know that he didn't die for his own sins. No one ever lived the perfect life he did. Our sins nailed him to the cross.

> *He didn't die for his own sins.*

Until we understand that we are the reason he had to die, we are not ready to be Christians. We should be the ones hanging. Can we face that fact, or will we look for something else to believe in that doesn't offend us? Something that lets us fit in with the world? Or something more intellectual? Or something we can earn with our good works? Or something we can do in our own power? Or something that overlooks our sins?

The cross strips us of our self-righteousness and of the false notion that we can earn our way to God by being good. The cross declares that all our efforts to reach God are not good enough. Our good works are like dirty rags[10] when it comes to getting back together with God. Instead, God the Son had to die to reconcile us to God the Father.

In fact, it is an insult to Christ's work on the cross to think that our good works can earn our way to God. He paid the ultimate price for our sins. How can we add to what Jesus did? Was his death insufficient? Our good works are nothing compared to the cross. Forgiveness and reunion with God are gifts. Our pride in our own efforts is defeated.

[10] Isaiah 64:6.

We lay down our pride; it dies with the cross. Only the humble can receive the cross.

The cross declares God's love more than anything else. Laying down one's life for another is the greatest act of love.[11] And it is shocking that the infinite, all-powerful God would become a man and die for us. Even more amazing is that he did not do it because we were good people but because we weren't. We were sinners who had chosen to run our own lives without God. We constantly broke the law of love. But he created us, loves us, and gladly gave his life for his priceless people.[12]

The cross proves how much he values you and how much he wants friendship with you. He wants to heal your shame and brokenness. He wants you to know you are accepted, not rejected. He wants to walk with you through the tough times. He wants to give your heart the security of knowing he is with you and cares for you. He wants to give you purpose for your life. He wants to make your life a beautiful reflection of his goodness. He wants you to enjoy using your gifts and abilities to love others. He wants to give you self-acceptance, confidence, and boldness. He wants to give you the freedom and happiness that comes from knowing you will spend eternity in a paradise of joyful community with God and his followers.

So now the question is this: what will you do with his cross? Will you accept his invitation to follow him? The next three chapters explain how to become a follower of Jesus.

Because of his love for you, he humbled himself to become a man. Because of his love for you, he endured hostility and rejection from the Jewish leaders. Because of his love for you, he let them mock him, spit upon him, and whip him. Because of his love for you, he let them convict

[11] John 15:13.
[12] Romans 5:8.

him like a criminal. Because of his love for you, he quietly listened as the crowd called for his crucifixion. Because of his love for you, he let them drive nails through his hands and feet. Because of his love for you, he felt his flesh tear at the nails while hanging on the cross. Because of his love for you, his entire body was racked with pain as he hung. Because of his love for you, he was ridiculed—even while he died. Because of his love for you, he slowly suffocated until he died. Because of his love for you, he gave his all.

For prayer and reflection

When you think about the cross, how does it affect you? Does the cross help you understand God's love for you?

Do you want forgiveness of your sins?

Do you want to become a follower of Jesus? The next three chapters explain how to do this.

Prayer

Prayer of openness to the gospel

God, I open my heart to you and ask you to plant the truth about your Son there. Help me know that your Son died for my sins. Thank you for proving your love for me through the cross. I am open to becoming a follower of Jesus.

CHAPTER 3

REPENTANCE: TURNING FROM YOUR OLD LIFE

Will You Admire Jesus or Follow Jesus?

NOW COMES THE time to respond to all that God has done and especially what the Son of God did on the cross. The cross is an invitation to turn from our old lives and follow Jesus. In return, he promises salvation, which is forgiveness of sins and a new eternal life with God. It is the life that our hearts long for. He pours his love out on us and gives us meaning, value, and fulfillment through an intimate relationship with him.

You begin to follow Jesus by repenting of your old ways, believing in Jesus' message of salvation, and surrendering your life to him. When you do this, you are saved! This chapter and the next two explain these three responses.

The process of rescuing us continues throughout our lives because he keeps on transforming us and making us one with him. In the first chapter, we learned that he wants to save us from being disconnected from himself—our Creator and Lover. He wants to recover the communion with him and with others that we lost; that is the meaning of salvation. He wants to set us free from our old lives, make us his children, and bring us into his kingdom.

But you must make the decision to follow him, not just admire him. Before we look at repentance, it will be helpful to discuss the problem of admiration.

Some people admire what Jesus taught, but they never respond to his invitation to follow him. They might deceive themselves into believing that they are in good standing with God because they admire Jesus and believe in the things he taught. But this is just a way of easing our consciences while keeping ourselves at a distance from him. We don't want to pay the price of actually following him, but we're afraid of deciding not to follow him. By admiring Jesus and believing he was good, we can tell ourselves that we have decided for God. But if we were truly honest with ourselves, we would see that we are living in the land of indecision. This is just a way to numb our consciences and avoid choosing.

It is like telling yourself you want to become a tennis player, but you don't spend the time and effort to do so. You buy a tennis racket, you talk about tennis with your friends, and you watch tennis on television, but you don't actually play tennis. You feel like you are involved with tennis because you admire it and talk about it. But you are not really a tennis player.

Jesus doesn't want admirers; he wants players. He wants to give you so much, but he can't unless you decide to follow

> **Jesus doesn't want admirers; he wants players.**

him. Admiration is really just a cowardly response to Jesus. Better to decide against him and become a pagan or better to try every other religion on earth than to simply admire Jesus. At least if you try paganism or other religions, they might eventually bring you around to Jesus.

For reflection

Do you admire Jesus but resist following him? Why?

Take Time to Consider Jesus

On the other hand, taking time to consider Jesus is not indecision. Considering what he taught and what he did on the cross is a good thing. Jesus said that we should count the cost before we decide to follow him.[1] It is like a driver who takes time to examine a map to see if he wants to make a trip. So before you decide to follow Jesus, take time to consider what he said and what he asks of you. This book should help you understand the cost.

Unfortunately, Christian leaders often ask people to decide to follow Jesus before they have considered him. Perhaps you have been at a church service or youth meeting, and at the end of the talk, the speaker gives a short salvation invitation followed by a prayer. The prayer usually goes something like this: "Jesus, I believe you are the Son of God and that you died for my sins. Please come into my life

---

[1] Luke 14:28.

and forgive my sins. I accept you as my Lord and Savior. I accept your gift of eternal life and thank you that I am going to heaven." Then the speaker tells those who prayed that prayer that they are now saved and going to heaven.

Perhaps you responded to a prayer like that, but nothing changed in your life. If so, you are like many others who respond but never experience salvation because they were not given the time and explanation to truly consider God's invitation to salvation. Did the invitation allow enough time for you to be convicted about your sins? Did you have enough time to think about whether you really wanted to turn

> *Jesus' life and death are an invitation to follow him.*

away from your old life? Did you have enough time to make the momentous decision to let Jesus be Lord of your life? Such matters deserve thoughtful and serious consideration. It takes time to make those decisions, and until you do, you are not able to receive God's salvation in Christ.

Jesus' life and death are an invitation to follow him—his teachings, his way of life, his love and submission to the Father, his way of treating people, and his way of suffering. This is the path to new life. Every other path leads to a dead end. He himself is life, and he promises to give true life to those who follow his narrow way. Your part is to decide whether to move in his direction or to move in another direction. His invitation to you is to choose to walk as he walked.

Following Jesus begins and continues with three responses: *repent, believe,* and *surrender.* You may not respond in that order, and you may even feel like it all happens at once, but all three responses will occur.

Sometimes the Bible says to believe, and you will be saved, but the word *believe* in the Bible includes repentance and surrender. If you were on a journey and figured out that the road you were on was leading you in the wrong direction, then first you would *repent* by turning back. Next, you would *believe* in another road, and finally you would *surrender* yourself to a new road by actually traveling down it.

You could sum up the whole experience by saying you *believed* in a new road, or you could name each of the three responses when you believed. In the Bible, Jesus and his disciples teach about salvation in the same way. They use only the term *believe* or *faith* in some passages and use words about *repentance* or *surrender* in other passages.[2]

This chapter explains repentance, and the next two chapters explain believing and surrendering.

For reflection

Did you say a prayer for salvation once, but it did not change your life? If so, did you take time to consider what it means to follow Jesus?

The Process of Repentance

The definition of *repentance* is to have a change of mind or heart that causes you to turn away from your old life.

> *He doesn't call you to stop sinning—that's impossible.*

Jesus and his apostles repeatedly taught that repentance was a requirement for salvation. When Jesus began his ministry,

---

[2] If you want to study this, you can begin with the following passages: Matthew 28:19; Mark 16:15–16; Luke 7:50; 14:27; 24:47; John 3:16; Acts 2:38; 3:19; 16:29–31; 20:21; 22:16; Romans 1:17; 10:9–10; and 1 Peter 3:21.

he declared, "The kingdom of God is near. Repent and believe the good news!"[3] He also said, "I have not come to call the righteous, but sinners to repentance."[4] After Jesus rose from the dead, he explained that now "repentance for forgiveness of sins would be proclaimed in His name to all the nations."[5] When Jesus' apostle Peter preached his first sermon to the crowds at Pentecost, his instruction to them was to repent and be baptized for the forgiveness of their sins.[6] The apostle Paul sums up his teaching by saying that people must turn to God in repentance and have faith in our Lord Jesus.[7]

So when God calls you, he calls you to repent. He doesn't call you to stop sinning—that is impossible. He calls you to decide to turn away from your old life, from sin and self, and turn to him. He will help you to get rid of your sin over time.

If God is calling you to follow him, then he will help you decide to turn away from your old life, but doing so may still be hard. You may be comfortable with your old life and may want to keep doing some sins. But he can help you choose.

The life of William Wilberforce is a good example of repentance. He was born in 1759 in Hull, England. He was gifted and ambitious, and at the age of twenty-one, he won a seat in the House of Commons in the English Parliament for his city. Soon his eloquence and gifting enabled him to win the prestigious seat for the County of Yorkshire at the young age of twenty-four. Wilberforce was enjoying the

---

[3] Mark 1:15 NIV.

[4] Luke 5:32 NIV.

[5] Luke 24:47.

[6] Acts 2:38.

[7] Acts 20:21.

high life and later admitted that his goals were advancing his own career and status.

But a friend of his, Isaac Milner, convinced him of the truth of Christianity. At this point, Wilberforce turned away from his old life of self-ambition. His quandary now was how to serve the Lord; should he serve in politics or as a minister? He chose politics and became the voice in England for the abolition of slavery. His powerful influence eventually led to the elimination of slavery in British territories. By giving his life to fighting injustice instead of seeking his own ambitions, Wilberforce demonstrated the true repentance that occurred in his heart when he first believed.

You may be afraid of what you will lose when you turn away from your old life. You may be afraid of losing some pleasures. You may think that following Jesus will be boring or a constant strain. You may be afraid of losing the admiration of your friends and relatives.

Let me be honest with you. You *will* lose some of these things (although following Jesus is not boring or a constant strain), but you will gain much more. That is why Jesus said we should count the cost. The things you lose are like a rotting bridge that you have been using to try to reach happiness or peace. The bridge may look good on the outside, but it is rotting from the inside out, and eventually the wood will turn to dust. Your friends, your abilities, your job, your pride, your money, your spouse, your children, your hobbies, your pleasures, your status, your brains, your muscles, your looks, your wisdom, your philosophy, your success, your pain, your self-pity, your defenses, your coping mechanisms, and the power of yourself are all rotting bridges if you depend on them for true life. You will never reach the other side, and you will eventually fall through.

Repent from trusting in these things. Some of these things are good; they are gifts from God, but they can only bring limited happiness at best. They cannot bring eternal life. Jesus said, "I am ... the life."[8] He is the only one you can trust for eternal life.

Repentance begins with sorrow in your heart.[9] If you have been convicted of sin as we discussed in chapter 1, then the next feeling in your heart should be sorrow. (Remember that sin is anything that breaks the law of love.) When you realize how much you have sinned, how often you have hurt people, and how you have continually rejected God, you should feel sorrow—maybe even shed tears.

If you haven't felt sorrow yet, then ask God to give you a true understanding of and sorrow for your sin. Give him some time, and it will begin to grip your heart. Sorrow for sin is a wonderful gift from God and should lead you to repentance and salvation.

Not all sorrow leads to repentance, however. Some have sorrow for their sins, but they stop there. They may think that sorrow is enough, but they don't really want to turn from their old lives. Some don't think they *can* turn away from their sins, and all they can do is be sorry. Others think their sins stop them from coming to God; they don't know that God desires people who know they are sinners.

Don't stop at sorrow. Let it lead your heart to repentance.

Be careful of half-hearted responses. Just feeling guilty and admitting your guilt is not repentance. Just conviction of sin is not repentance. Regret for your "mistakes" is not repentance. And regret for your sins is not repentance. Sorrow by itself is not repentance. Asking for forgiveness is not repentance. Asking God to save you from your sins is not repentance. Fear of God's judgment is not repentance.

---

[8] John 14:6.
[9] 2 Corinthians 7:10.

None of these by themselves include an actual choice to turn away from your old life—that is true repentance.

Repentance is a matter of the heart. It is a matter of giving up your hold on your own way of living. Let go of your grip on your old ways and on the way you run your life. If you have a love affair with your old life, it is time to break up. Your old lover is ruining you and keeping you from the infinite Lover. Let the truth about your sins sink into your heart, and when you do, that reality will show you your need for God.

> *If you have a love affair with your old life, it is time to break up.*

Remember the deep longing and loneliness that live in your heart. Remember how your separation from God leaves you without peace, meaning, and hope. Remember how much God longs to be close to you and to show you how much he loves you. He wants to adopt you as his own child. Let these truths move your heart to turn from its usual ways.

Why would you want to continue down your old road when it only leads to an eternity away from God and his love and blessings for you? If you don't turn away, you will spend forever in misery.

You will find new life if you decide to turn away from all the ways you have sought happiness without God: abilities, possessions, people, power, sex, sports, entertainment, or hobbies. And you need to turn away from the sins that come from inside your heart: anger, lust, pride, self-exaltation, self-sufficiency, rebellion, hatred, greed, dishonesty, unkindness, disrespect, neglect of the needy, selfishness, envy, gossip, fighting, arrogance, boasting, revenge, violence, jealousy, gluttony, and all the other dark and evil things you do.[10]

You even need to start turning away from unforgiveness and grudges against people who have hurt you. We've all been hurt, but now is the time to let go. And finally, you need to start turning away from running your own life. All these sins damage your soul and keep you from the one who can give you true life.

Take time to count the cost. Take time to let repentance fill your heart so that you truly do want to turn away. Ask God to give you a repentant heart. Then you can wholeheartedly choose to turn away from your old life.

The good news about repentance is that when you decide to turn away from your old life, it does not mean that you are choosing to stop sinning. You do not have the power to do so. You might be able to stop doing many of your sins, but until God saves you, you will still have a corrupt nature and a deep loneliness that constantly nurtures sin in your heart.

When you repent, you are just choosing to no longer go in the old direction and no longer set your heart on the old things. When you believe in Jesus and surrender to him, then he will help you to stop sinning, to stop breaking the law of love. This is a key difference between Christianity and all other religions: God promises to do the work in you. You do not have to make yourself good. He will send his Spirit to dwell in you and restore your heart so you can love God and others.

Don't make the mistake of thinking that you have to clean up your life before you come to God. You can't do it. You can only come to God as a dirty sinner who has decided to turn away from your old life.

---

[10] Many of these sins and others are found in Romans 1:29–32 and Galatians 5:19–21.

So when you repent, believe, and surrender to Jesus, you will not sin as often. You may even think you are winning the battle in your own power. But actually a mysterious blend of God's power flowing into you enables you to stop breaking the law of love. In fact, God gives you the desire to continually repent and turn to him. God convicts you of sin; you do not convict yourself. From beginning to end, it is all God's initiative and work. You just respond to him, and he will enable you to respond.

If you are not ready to turn away from your old life, then you are not ready to receive salvation. But you can continue to ask God to help make your heart ready. And you can spend time with Christians, go to church, and keep your heart open to God's work.

When you are ready to repent, it may be helpful to list your sins. Write down the ways you break the law of love toward God and others. List your sinful attitudes as well as your sinful actions and habits. Everyone has his or her own combination of sinfulness. When you repent, tell God that you don't want your old life and are turning away from it, that you are choosing against all your old ways, that you are a sinner, and that you are coming to him to make you clean. Tell him that you are changing roads to follow his road to love and community with him and others.

For reflection and prayer

Where are you in the process of repentance?

Do you have sorrow for your sins? Do you have the desire to turn away from them?

Are you ready to decide to turn away from your sins?

Consider the prayers below. Pray one if it reflects your heart.

Prayers

Prayer for sorrow

God, I open my heart to you and give you permission to touch me and to give me true sorrow and remorse for my sins. I want to know and feel the impact of my sins on myself, on others, and on you.

Prayer for the desire to repent

God, I open my heart to you and ask you to give me a heart of repentance. Let my sins smell like a pile of manure to me. Let my old life be like a bad taste in my mouth. Work in my mind and heart so that I choose to turn away from my old life and turn to you.

Prayer of actual repentance

God, I don't want my old life, and I'm turning away from it. I now choose against all my old ways. They include (list ones you are aware of), and I am no longer trusting in them. I am turning away from being the boss of my life. I am a sinner, and I am coming to you to make me clean. I am changing directions to follow your road to restoration of love and community with you and others.

Visit Road To New Life Ministries
for growing in the ways of Jesus

On Twitter: @RoadNewLifeMin
On The Web: www.TheRoadToNewLife.com

CHAPTER 4

BELIEF: ACCEPTING
THE TRUTH
FOR YOURSELF

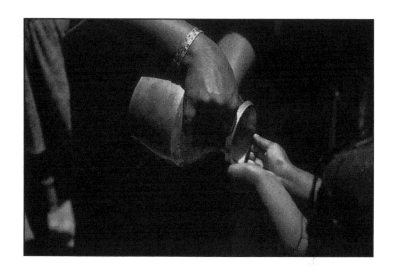

Openness, Hearing, and Faith

IN CHAPTER 3, we saw that following Jesus can be summed up in three responses: *repentance, belief,* and *surrender.* This chapter is about believing or faith (the two words are interchangeable), although faith can also refer to all three responses.

In chapter 1, you learned that God wants to unite with you in love. He wants to bring you into a kingdom community of love with other followers of God. But your sin

39

of breaking the law of love for God and others is blocking this. In chapter 2, you learned that he provided a way for you to receive forgiveness of sins and reunion with God. He sent his Son to die for your sins. In chapter 3, you learned that he is calling you to repent of your old life because you are breaking the law of love. Now he is calling you to believe in his Son so he can set you free from your old life, unite with you, and bring you into his kingdom of love and wholeness.

God wants you to hear all these messages because faith comes through hearing God's Word.[1] These are the words of God calling you to himself. He wants to be with you. He wants to put his life and his Spirit in your heart. He wants to set you free. He wants to give you a new heart that will experience his peace, joy, and love in spite of the difficulties of life. He wants to show you the meaning of your life and give you a purpose for living.

But your heart must be open to hearing God's message. If your heart is open, he will begin to give you faith.

As you read this book, how are you responding? What is happening in your heart? Is it open? Can you hear God calling you? You have a choice either to listen or to close your ears and heart. Listen with your heart as well as your mind. Christianity does not contradict reason, but it does transcend it.

> *As you read this book, how are you responding? What is happening in your heart? Is it open?*

Your heart has its own thoughts about all this. Let God's words touch and embrace you. Let them sink all the way down into your spirit. "Today if you hear His voice, do not harden your hearts."[2] It is your choice whether to harden

---

[1] See Romans 10:17.

[2] Hebrews 3:15.

your heart against his voice or to let his words break into your heart and spread his life and light into every corner. Jesus said, "He who has ears to hear, let him hear."[3] When Jesus taught in Israel, he lamented,

> For the hearts of these people are hardened,
> and their ears cannot hear,
> and they have closed their eyes—
> so their eyes cannot see,
> and their ears cannot hear,
> and their hearts cannot understand,
> and they cannot turn to me
> and let me heal them.[4]

If your ears cannot hear, if they cannot open up to what God is saying, then ask him for help. Ask him for ears to hear. If you desire him, then tell him, and he will show you.

Our roles are not to figure out ultimate truth with our own minds; our roles are to hear, consider, and receive by faith. He has revealed the truth. He sent his Son to be born in a specific place and time in history. Jesus lived and served and died and rose again. This is God's revelation of truth and salvation. He did not expect us to figure this out ourselves. In his mercy he reveals it to us in Jesus and asks us to receive it. Do God's words resonate as truth in your heart? Do you sense his calling you? Can you "hear" that Jesus is your salvation? Do you sense the dawning of faith in your heart?

---

[3] Matthew 11:15.
[4] Matthew 13:15 NLT.

For reflection and prayer

Is your heart open to hearing God? If not, why not?

Do you have anger or a grudge against God that is blocking you from being open to him? If so, can you talk to him about it, then ask him to help you let go of it as much as possible?

Has a Christian or a church hurt you? Is this keeping you from God? Can you forgive them?

Does a grudge or frustration about life or another person block you from being open to God? If so, can you talk to God about it, then ask him to help you let go of it as much as possible?

Prayer

Prayer for spiritual hearing

God, I want to be able to hear your words. I want my heart to be open to truly hear and believe the message of the gospel. Open my spiritual ears and help me to believe. I open up to you and ask you to help me hear you calling me.

What God Asks You to Believe

God is asking you to believe the gospel, which is his message of salvation. Believe that Jesus was the Son of God, which means that he was and is divine. "For in Him [Christ] all the fullness of Deity dwells in bodily form."[5] The apostle John referred to Jesus as the Word and stated that "the Word was God."[6] Jesus Christ was more than just a man; he was

---

[5] Colossians 2:9.

[6] John 1:1.

God in the flesh. Since he was divine and sinless, he was the perfect and infinite sacrifice for the sins of all people.

God is asking you to believe that Jesus took your place on the cross—that he died for your sins.[7] You have failed to love God and others, and you should have died for your own sins. But Jesus died in your place.

He is asking you to believe that he is offering you forgiveness of sins if you will repent, believe, and surrender to him. If you take these three steps, then you can know that every sin you ever committed or will commit has already been paid for. There is no more condemnation for those who believe.[8]

He is asking you to believe that Jesus rose from the dead and ascended into heaven, thus conquering sin and death. When you believe in Jesus, you do not need to fear death anymore. Jesus has defeated the fear of death. Now God gives you new and eternal life through his Son, and this life begins the moment you believe (and repent and surrender). This is the gospel.

> *You immediately enter the kingdom of God and join his community of love, truth, and freedom.*

When you believe, you immediately enter the kingdom of God and join his community of love, truth, and freedom. He deposits in you a deep wellspring of living water that flows from the life of God himself.

He is asking you to believe that all of this is for you. Believe that he is the giver of life and receive it.

And when he says *believe*, he does not want you to simply agree in your mind that it is true. He wants you to

---

[7] 1 Corinthians 15:3.

[8] See Romans 8:1.

believe in your heart that it is true[9] and true for you. He also wants you to believe in the sense of trusting him with your life and following him, which is the topic of the next chapter on surrender. The point now is for you to believe the truth of the message of salvation through Jesus and to receive it for yourself.

Actually, you are receiving Jesus himself into your heart. You are not just receiving words; you are receiving a person.

The life of Marie Sklodowska provides a good illustration of believing and receiving. She was born in Poland in 1867. She was very bright and excelled in school. She wanted to become a scientist, but the Russians who ruled Poland at the time wouldn't allow her to study in her country's universities. Eventually, she was able to move to Paris to study at the prestigious University of Sorbonne. She excelled in chemistry and physics and won a scholarship.

Pierre Curie, the director of a laboratory where Marie worked, was attracted to her and asked her to marry him. She said no. Marrying him would mean giving up her dream of returning to her homeland Poland. Their friendship grew and again he asked her to marry him. Again she said no. She was not romantically attracted to him. He continued to woo her and asked her a third time. Finally, she said yes. She finally believed that he was the one for her, and she was willing to receive him into her heart.

Their friendship turned into a deep love, and they worked together as pioneers in physics. In 1903 Marie and Pierre, along with Henri Becquerel, were awarded the Nobel Prize in physics for their discoveries on radiation. Madam Curie became the first woman ever awarded a Nobel Prize. Radiation became a valuable tool for the advancement of medical science and thus a great benefit for mankind.

[9] Romans 10:9–10

Your relationship with God is like a romance. God is pursuing you. He is courting you and speaking words of love to you. He is hoping you open your heart and believe that his heart is for you. He wants to give you true life. Believe in his Son and receive him into your heart.

For reflection

Can you believe that Jesus is the divine Son of God? If this is a challenge, ask God for help and understanding.

Can you believe that Jesus died on the cross for your sins? If this is a challenge, ask God for help and understanding.

Things That Hold You Back from Believing

As with any new, important relationship, you may have fears and doubts about believing and receiving Jesus.

One fear many people have is giving up things that they know are not good, such as certain activities or relationships. They know that if they believe in Jesus, then they will need to follow his teachings, which would mean some sacrifice. But remember, you are giving up things that are damaging you spiritually. Maybe they can make your life more comfortable for a while, but if you are willing to give up that comfort and go through some discomfort, then you will find the true life you really desire.

Athletes must sacrifice time and activities and go through difficult training in order to reach their goals. Likewise, you cannot find peace and happiness unless you are willing to sacrifice the activities or relationships that hold you back from believing God's message of salvation.

Another fear, similar to the previous one, is that you will not have any more pleasure. You may think you have to give up earthly pleasures and live a dry, moral life. But this is not true. Not only does following Jesus have many pleasures, but he also gives new meaning and enjoyment to the healthy pleasures you had before you believed. You will begin to find new pleasure in music, recreation, hobbies, and relationships. This is because you are now grounded in and being filled with the peace and love of God's life inside you. This new life can now flow into everything you do.

Another reason you may not want to believe is that you don't want to give up your own beliefs and viewpoints. Your philosophies may conflict with Jesus' teachings. Or your family or culture may have planted conflicting beliefs in you. Are you clinging to your own beliefs just because you don't want to think you are wrong or because it makes it easier to fit in with your social group? Instead, you have to ask yourself, *Which beliefs will lead me to the source of true life and all that is good?* Whose truth will bring you into relationship with God, yours or Jesus'?

You will find it helpful to read about Jesus' life in one or more of the four biographies ("Gospels") of Jesus in the New Testament. The names of those books are Matthew, Mark, Luke, and John. (I recommend reading Luke first, but you can start with any of them.) Ask yourself if his truth is greater than yours. If it is and if you honestly want truth and life, then your choice is clear.

Another reason you may hesitate to believe is that you may be asking yourself, *How can I be sure this is true?* The answer is that you can't be sure in your mind, and you may or may not be sure in your heart. Sometimes God gives people clear confidence in their hearts before they believe, and sometimes it comes after they believe.

Making sure is usually motivated by our human desires to be in control or to know what will happen ahead of time. But it gets in the way of intimate relationships. This is where faith plays its part. With another person, your leap of faith may or may not turn out well. But you will never know, and you will never find love unless you make the leap of faith. It is the same with following Jesus because it is a relationship, except that his love is perfect and reliable. You need to give up your requirement to make sure if you want to follow Jesus and enjoy a communion of love with God.

The reason you can't be sure is because your natural mind is not a spiritual thing, and God communicates primarily with our spirits as well as our minds. Spiritual things need to be spiritually received.[10]

On the other hand, God created our minds and respects them. That is why he provided much evidence that the gospel is true. The leap of faith is not blind or irrational. We have the words of Jesus to rely on. And God gave us the writings of eyewitnesses in the New Testament to help us. He placed the events of Jesus' life in a specific historical setting so that we could know that the writings fit with history. You can find more evidence for Jesus and the gospel in the many good books on the subject. [11]

God has not given us absolute, logical proof that the gospel is true. However, there is enough evidence to deserve our attention and consideration. The unusually profound teachings of Jesus alone should be enough to open our hearts to consider believing in him.

But the evidence only takes us so far. Soren Kierkegaard, a famous Christian author and philosopher, said that evidence for the gospel may be enough to take us to the edge of the chasm, but we still have to make the leap. God wants us to come to him by faith, not just by logic. He wants a relationship of love, not just an intellectual agreement on spiritual truth. And faith is the leap towards love.

---

[10] See 1 Corinthians 2:14.

[11] For example, see Lee Strobel's *The Case for Christ*, C. S. Lewis's *Mere Christianity*, and Josh McDowell's *More Than a Carpenter*.

With respect to being sure in your heart, maybe you will have strong assurance that this is all true before you believe, or you may have very little. As long as you have the desire to believe, it is okay. Everyone has to

> *Faith is the leap toward love.*

make his or her own leap; it is just a little harder for some. Wherever you are is okay. And it is okay to take your time and let his words sink in until you have the courage to take the leap.

As I mentioned above, you will find it helpful to read about Jesus' life and teachings in the four Gospels in the New Testament. Tell God your thoughts and ask your questions. Find someone you can talk to. Then, when your heart begins to have conviction that it is true, take the leap. Choose to believe. You may not be completely sure, but when you leap without being completely sure, then you are learning how to do "faith." God will catch you when you take the leap, and you will find your true home in his open arms of love.

Remember that it is human to doubt and that many have doubts when they make the leap of faith. Even after the leap, most Christians have doubts at times about whether this is all true and even about whether God is really there. So faith and doubt can coexist. You can be honest with God about your doubts and ask him to help you. And they don't need to stop you from following Jesus.

In the gospel of Mark, a father came to Jesus and asked him to heal his son if he could. Jesus chided him for saying "if" because he didn't believe. The father replied, "I do believe; help my unbelief."[12] And Jesus healed his son. So it is okay to ask God to help you with your unbelief. God

---

[12] Mark 9:24.

48

will honor you for the faith that you have now. He will give you more faith as you walk with him.

For reflection and prayer

Do you have beliefs that block you from believing the gospel? Can you talk to God about those beliefs and ask him to help you know if your beliefs are true? Also, are they good reasons to be closed to God?

Do you have other barriers, such as doubts or fears, that interfere with believing the gospel? Can you talk to God about them?

Consider the prayers below. Pray one if it reflects your heart.

Prayers

Prayer for help in giving up things

God, I admit that I am afraid to give up some things in my life to believe in your Son. Help me to see that it is better to give them up and give me the strength to do so.

Prayer for help in letting go of old beliefs

God, I'm not sure I want to give up my own beliefs to believe in your Son. Help me to see which truths are better and help me to let go of my ego attachment to my own beliefs. I truly want to see the truth and follow it.

Prayer for help to know if the gospel is true

God, I am unsure about whether the message of salvation is true. Help me to listen spiritually and tune in to your spiritual channel. Give my heart the conviction that the gospel is true so I can make the leap of faith.

Prayer of belief in the gospel

God, I am willing to make the leap of faith. I believe that Jesus Christ was your divine Son who came to earth and lived a perfect life of love. I believe he died on the cross for my sins, and I receive the forgiveness of sins you are offering me. I believe that Jesus rose from the dead and ascended into heaven, thus conquering sin and death. I believe that you give an eternal life of love with you and your followers in your kingdom to those who repent, believe, and follow.

And Lord, when I say, "I believe," I don't just mean that I agree in my mind that these things are true. I mean that I believe in my heart and that I receive these truths and your Son into my heart. And even though I may have some unbelief, I still believe, and I ask you to help me with my unbelief.

CHAPTER 5

SURRENDER: LETTING JESUS BE YOUR LEADER

Count the Cost and Follow His Voice

IN CHAPTER 3, we learned that following Jesus can be summed up in three responses: *repentance, belief,* and *surrender.* This chapter is about surrender, which is actually the completion of faith. Surrender is the same as "entrusting" or "deciding to follow."

Surrender is the final stage in the process of salvation. We discussed the other stages in chapters 1 (conviction),

2 (Jesus' death and resurrection for us), 3 (repentance), and 4 (belief). Remember that salvation is the process of God's forgiving your sins and bringing you into an eternal communion of love with God and others. Salvation is leaving the way of eternal darkness, coming into God's kingdom, and being adopted as a child of God.

But before you can be saved, you need to decide whether you are going to surrender your life to him. Scripture states, "If you confess with your mouth that Jesus is Lord and believe in your heart that God raised him from the dead, you will be saved."[1]

Hopefully, you have repented of your sins and believed that Jesus is the Son of God who died for your sins. But the salvation process is incomplete until you decide to let Jesus be the leader or lord of your life. Jesus is calling to you, "Follow me."[2] Will you follow him?

This means giving up being boss of your own life. This is the hardest step for many people to take. We all like being in charge of our lives; it is not natural for us to surrender control to someone else. It may seem scary. You can't be sure what will happen. This is the cost of becoming a Christian.

Actually, Jesus will be a much better leader of your life than you are. He is all-powerful and all-knowing, and he loves you more than you love yourself. He leads with kindness and a servant's heart. He listens to you and values what

> *Jesus will be a much better leader of your life than you are.*

you think and feel. He created you and knows what is best for your soul. He will be the Good Shepherd of your life.

---

[1] Romans 10:9 NLT.

[2] See Matthew 8:22; 16:24; John 10:27.

Surrender is not about cleaning up your life before you are saved; rather, it is deciding to start following Jesus and the way he lived and letting him clean up your life. And the way he lived was not the way other people lived. He did not promote power, wealth, popularity, following rules, or higher learning as the way to abundant life. He sacrificed, he served, and he forgave. He lived a life of love. As a result, he not only lived in great joy and peace but also accepted suffering. Once you decide to start following Jesus, God will give you his Spirit to enable you to follow Jesus' example.

This is why Jesus said to "count the cost" before you decide to follow him. "You cannot be my disciple [i.e., a Christian] if you do not carry your own cross and follow me. But don't begin until you count the cost."[3] Take some time to consider what you are doing. Don't just make an emotional decision, thinking all your problems will be solved if you become a Christian. Your life will not be all happiness and joy. Instead, it is like a marriage: you will have challenges and hard times. But it will be the best relationship in your life, and you will find real life. It will far surpass your old one.

The story of a troubled Russian girl is a good illustration of surrender.

> Natasha was thirteen when the trouble came to her family. It was then that her uncle moved into her parents' apartment, bringing a lifestyle of heavy drinking and violence. He regularly beat his niece. Her parents, often drinking too, were too frightened to intervene. Having suffered a brutal assault, Natasha eventually ran away from home.[4]

[3] Luke 14:27–28 NLT.

[4] Natasha's real name has been changed to protect her anonymity. This story can be found at http://www.unicef.org/russia/protection_5177.html.

Natasha was homeless and lived on the street. Through the police, she found a shelter for underage girls. Now she had a choice: she could keep her "freedom," stay on the streets, and go anywhere she wanted; or she could surrender her freedom and live in the shelter. The shelter provided people who cared, a roof over her head, food to eat, and even psychological help. She surrendered to the shelter.

She sometimes thought about her old freedom and even ran away from the shelter twice. But she came back. A psychologist helped her overcome her emotional issues, and, with the help of tutors, she became a good student. She moved into a boarding school and dreams of one day becoming a psychologist to help others like her.

Until you surrender to Jesus, you are like a homeless child who has grown hungry and tired and is trying to find a place to rest. Then someone comes up to you and offers you a home, food, and peace. Now you must count the cost. You can keep your freedom and turn down the offer. Or you can give up your old freedom, become part of a new family, and live in a new home. If you accept the offer, your new freedom will be much better than your old freedom, which was only a dead end.

If you decide to follow Jesus, you are choosing to join his family, live in his kingdom, and let him be your King. And the new land you will live in will be far bigger and better than your old place, which was really just a prison.

Surrender means not only that you believe that Jesus is the right road but also that you are actually going to start down that road. You are deciding to begin to let him lead you. Just believing that Jesus is the right road doesn't help unless you are going to follow the road.

Surrender means you are giving him permission to be leader of your mind, heart, and will—in other words, your whole self. It means he is leader over your hobbies, habits, entertainment, money, sexuality, image, status, career, attitudes, and especially relationships. It means that your heart is no longer set on the things of this world but on him and on the spiritual values and realities he shows you. It means that you are deciding to start following what he taught.

But remember, he is not asking you to reform your life *before* you come to him. He is asking you to turn your heart away from your old life and to look to him to give you a new life and new heart. Then you will be able to obey and love him, and he will transform your life.

Obviously, you will not be able to completely surrender your life to Jesus at the beginning. You cannot fully comprehend surrender yet. In fact, you are not even *able* to surrender all of yourself. That will take the rest of your life. You are just making an initial surrender. You are starting. You are giving him permission to start being your lord, your leader, your shepherd. When you do, he will give you salvation.

So this means that you must exercise your will and make a choice. Don't be like some who are afraid to actually make a decision, even when it seems right. That is spiritual cowardice. If you have heard him calling in your heart, have been convicted of your sin, have counted the cost, and are willing to repent and believe, then take the plunge. He is moving in your heart to give you courage to surrender and follow. Let your heart join with his and give yourself to him.

You declare your decision to give yourself to Jesus when you are baptized. Water baptism has many meanings, but one of the central meanings is that in baptism you die to yourself and surrender yourself to God in Christ as the water covers you. Then you are resurrected to new life in Christ as you come out of the water.[5] Baptism is the way of physically

---

[5] See Romans 6:3–6.

experiencing the spiritual reality you are going through in salvation. It will be an important experience for you. [6]

For reflection and prayer

Do you resist the idea of following Jesus' teachings and letting him be leader of your life? If so, why? Can you talk to God about your resistance?

Compare what you are giving up to what you are gaining if you decide to follow Jesus.

Don't Put It Off!

Some people would rather ignore God's voice for now and live how they want to live, then follow Jesus someday when they are done with their own way of living. But what if your heart gets hard as time goes on? What if you get more and more entrenched in your own path? What if it gets harder and harder to *decide* to follow Jesus? How do you know what will happen in your heart? Will you be able to hear him next time? How many times will God call to you to follow him? Remember the Scripture from chapter 4: "Today if you hear His voice, do not harden your hearts."[7]

Furthermore, how do you know when you will die? You *will* die. You just don't know when. You hear of people dying before their time every day. Perhaps you had a friend or relative who died earlier than expected. If you live your life as if you are not going to die, then you are living in denial. Let the reality of your death rattle your heart so you can

---

[6] If you were baptized as an infant, then you will need to decide if you want to be baptized again or if you want to have a public declaration confirming your baptism. Christian traditions have different views on which to do.

[7] Hebrews 3:15.

hear God. The specter of your death is a gift from God to inspire you to get serious about your life. All your anxiety about life should move you to seek God.

When I was twenty-three, I went on a raft trip with some friends. The river was challenging, but I had been down it a few weeks before with a friend so I felt confident. We put the raft in the same place as before, just above a rough set of rapids. The river was higher this time because of more snow-melt. We made it through

> *The specter of your death is a gift from God to inspire you to get serious.*

the tougher rapids, and we were almost out of the challenging section of the river when we went over a rock. A few weeks earlier, the rock had been visible because the river was lower, so we had gone around it. This time we couldn't see it because water was flowing over it, and we went right over the top of it. It was like a little waterfall, and our raft landed hard. I was sitting in back, and the water bounced me out of the raft and into the swirling water near the rock.

The water coming over the rock created a "Maytag" effect so the water kept circling round and round. I was caught in this circle. The water pulled me under and down, but eventually I came back up and just barely caught a breath of air. But the Maytag effect pulled me back down again, and I was getting a little scared. Eventually, I came back up again and caught another breath of air, but I was exhausted. My body was fighting every moment with all its strength. My sister was looking back from the raft downstream and crying because she could not see me. The water pulled me back down, and I knew I was out of breath. I did not think I would get back to the top in time to get some air. Now I thought I was going to die. It seemed strange to die this way, although it wasn't particularly painful. I stopped struggling and let my body go limp, expecting this was the end.

I'm not sure how, but my body got kicked out of the Maytag effect. The river carried me underwater (I don't know why I didn't run out of breath) for about another hundred feet. Then I finally came back up and knew I was safe. I looked to the sky and shouted, "I'm alive!" I just floated along, enjoying my "second" life.

This experience shattered any illusions I had about a guaranteed long life. I knew I could die at any moment. Even though I had been a Christian for several years, this event changed my life. Following God in Christ became the central motivation of my life. I was willing to surrender other things to draw near to God.

> *Your life is precious to God. Don't waste it.*

Your life is precious to God. Don't waste it. God is the source of life and wants to give you true life. No matter how broken you are or how bad a sinner you are, he loves you and wants you. He offers freedom, peace, security, purpose, and a close relationship with himself through Jesus. Soon your life on earth will be over. What holds you back from following his voice?

God will judge every life one day. How will God judge you if you ignore his voice and turn away from his salvation and gift of new life? If you choose to live away from him on earth, he will not force you to live with him in eternity. Instead, you will spend an unhappy eternity away from him.

What are you really giving up if you decide to follow him? Remember that all the things of this world that you desire more than God—money, possessions, power, control, influence, popularity, looks, image, sensual pleasure, family, career, success, status, achievement, security—will all be gone when you die.[8] And none of them satisfies the deep hole in your heart where God should be. These things keep you from the Creator, who made you, loves you, and wants to live inside you. He can make your heart flow with rivers of living water.[9]

Jim Elliot, a famous missionary martyr, said before his death, "He is no fool, who gives what he cannot keep, to gain what he cannot lose."[10] You are giving up an unsatisfying life to gain true, eternal life. Surrender to Jesus and his love.

For reflection and prayer

Do you believe that you could die at any time?

What will your eternal fate be if you stay on your current path? What will it be if you follow Jesus?

Are you ready to surrender your life to Jesus?

Prayers

Prayer for help to surrender

God, I am having a hard time giving up control of my life to You. I need Your help. Please give me the faith to surrender to You and decide to begin following You. I open myself up to You to work in me.

Prayer to surrender to Jesus and receive salvation

Lord Jesus, I have taken the time to count the cost of following you, and I want to begin to follow. I give up being in charge of my own life. I give up my control of everything, including my hobbies, habits, entertainment, money,

---

[8] See Romans 6:19–21

[9] John 7:38

[10] George Sweeting, *Who Said That?* (Chicago: Moody Press, 1995), 88.

sexuality, image, status, career, and especially relationships. I surrender them all to you and accept you as leader over my whole life. Help me to continue to more fully surrender everything to you.

I now fully receive you as my Savior and Lord. Fill me with your Holy Spirit.

Now that I have received the gospel with repentance, belief, and surrender, I thank you for my salvation. (This assumes you have prayed the prayers for repentance and belief at the end of chapters 3 and 4.) Thank you for eternal life. Thank you for adopting me as your child, bringing me into your kingdom community, and uniting me with you and your followers. Thank you for baptism, in which I will experience this new reality.

**Visit Road To New Life Ministries
for growing in the ways of Jesus**

On Twitter: @RoadNewLifeMin
On The Web: www.TheRoadToNewLife.com

A SUMMARY OF THE ROAD TO NEW LIFE

THIS CHAPTER IS a summary of the first five chapters. It is a helpful way to remember the essentials of finding new life. You can remember the five elements with the acronym SCRuBS, as in "Jesus scrubs us clean": S is for sin, C is for Christ, R is for repentance, B is for belief, and S is for surrender.

This chapter also contains the prayers at the end of each previous chapter for accepting this new life in Christ. If you

---

Permission is granted for unlimited use, reproduction, storage, transmission, and adaptation of Chapter 6.

have said these prayers and meant them from your heart, then you are saved and are an eternal member of God's kingdom community.

Chapter 1—Love, Sin, and Separation

God is a perfect Trinity who created the universe and humans to display and experience his love and power. He wanted to have an intimate friendship with humans—his children—and he wanted them to have perfect community with each other.

But humans gave in to the prideful temptation of becoming like God. Our hearts became corrupted and disconnected from God. We lost the ability to love God, love others, love ourselves, and live truly good lives. We became infected with guilt, shame, and rebellion. In others words, we fell and became sinners. And now our hearts have a big hole where God should be. We try to fill it with other things, but we can't find peace, truth, meaning, value, freedom, or love.

But God still desires to be close to us. He values us and wants to make us whole.

The gospel is God's invitation to unite with you. But you must first believe that you really are a sinner—that you do not love God and others as you should. All of us fall short of this standard. Also, your sins separate you from God, and you need him to rescue you.

God will not force you to accept his gospel and be with him. If you reject him, then you will spend eternity away from him. This is hell, and you will be trapped in misery and unhappiness forever.

Prayer confessing that you are convicted that you are a sinner

God, I realize you created me to love you and love others. I confess that I do not do this as I should. I have dishonored you by not letting you be Lord of my life. I have been selfish in my relationships with others, and I have hurt others. I know I have pride, anger, and unbelief. I try to satisfy myself with other pleasures instead of with you. I confess the other sins you have convicted me of: (Tell God all the sins you are aware of.) I know I am separated from you, and I need you to rescue me. Please lead me to salvation.

Chapter 2—The Story of God Saving His People

After the fall humans became more and more corrupt. But God did not give up on them. He still loved them greatly, and he devised a plan to bring them back to himself. He chose a man named Abraham and promised to bless all people through him. Later, he gave to a man named Moses, one of Abraham's descendants, commands to guide people in how to love God and love others.

But Abraham's descendants continually turned away from God. God sent other nations to conquer them so they would turn back to him. This cycle repeated several times.

Later, he promised one of the kings of Abraham's descendants, David, that he would give him a never-ending kingdom. God also promised through prophets that he would give them a Messiah to save them.

But the people continued to turn away from God, and he allowed several more nations to conquer them. It looked like God's plan to reunite with humans was not working.

During the Roman occupation in the first century AD, a Jew from Nazareth named Jesus began teaching that the kingdom of God had finally come. He taught that we should love all people, even our enemies. We should forgive those who hurt us. We should help the needy and give to others. We should not focus on wealth or being popular with everyone.

Jesus was a living example of his own teaching. He loved all who came to him, even the people society had rejected. He did great miracles and healed many people out of his love for them. He promised peace and joy to all who would follow him. He declared that he was the Way, the truth, and the life. He was the Messiah promised by the Jewish prophets centuries earlier.

But the Jewish leaders were jealous of Jesus' popularity. So they had him crucified. But he rose from the dead! He appeared to his followers, then ascended into heaven.

Jesus died on the cross for your sins. He took your place. You don't have to earn your way to God; he offers it as a gift. And by his resurrection, he defeated death and offers you new life. This is the incredible good news. Now he invites you to become his follower by repenting of your old life, believing, and surrendering to him.

He not only invites the broken, the lost, the needy, the lonely, the abused, and the rejected, but he also invites all who desire God. He values you and wants to heal your shame and your pain. He offers the gift of forgiveness of sins and a new life with God. He offers peace, satisfaction, truth, meaning, joy, and abundant life deep inside. And he offers a community of love for all eternity.

Prayer of openness to the gospel

God, I open my heart to you and ask you to plant the truth about your Son there. Help me to know that your Son died for my sins. Thank you for proving your love for me through the cross. I am open to becoming a follower of Jesus.

Chapter 3—Repentance: Turning from Your Old Life

Now you have the opportunity to respond to all God has done, especially Jesus' life and death on the cross. He is giving you an invitation. He wants to give you a new eternal life of peace and joy and meaning, but first you must decide whether you want to follow his Son. You can begin to follow Jesus by repenting of your old life, believing in Jesus' message of salvation, and surrendering your life to him.

But following him is not the same as admiring him. Many people admire Jesus but don't actually follow him. He wants to give you so much, but he can't unless you decide to follow his teachings and his example.

Before you decide to begin to follow Jesus, you need to take time to consider what he is asking of you. Perhaps you said a prayer for salvation in the past, but nothing changed in your life. Maybe the problem was that you did not take time to seriously consider repentance, belief, and surrender.

Repentance is the first step. It means turning away from your old life. Repentance begins with sorrow for your sins.

Turning away from your old life is part of the cost of following Jesus. Consider this cost before you decide to follow him.

Repentance includes turning away from all the ways in which you do not love God and love others. This includes turning away from pride, selfishness, dishonesty, materialism, indulging lusts, and unkindness. And it means letting go of being in charge of your own life. It does not mean you have to stop sinning; that is impossible. Instead, it means you turn away and come to Jesus just as you are and ask him to help you replace your sins with love.

Prayer of actual repentance

God, I don't want my old life, and I am turning away from it. I now choose against all my old ways. They include (list ones you are aware of), and I am no longer trusting in them. I am turning away from being boss of my own life. I am a sinner and am coming to you to make me clean. I am changing directions to follow your road to restoration of love and community with you and others.

Chapter 4—Belief: Accepting the Truth for Yourself

The next step toward salvation is belief. God wants to speak to your heart and help you believe the gospel, the good news. But you have to keep your heart open to him so you can hear. Be sure to listen with your heart as well as with your mind.

If you are not open to God, it might be because you have a grudge against him. If you do, you should talk to him about it. Tell him how you feel and ask him to help you let go of it.

God is asking you to believe his message of salvation that Jesus is the Son of God who died for your sins, that he rose from the dead and conquered sin and death. If you repent, believe in him, and surrender to him, then your sins are forgiven, and you will have new eternal life that begins immediately in his kingdom community.

He is asking you to believe and receive this gospel and salvation for yourself.

Maybe you have barriers to believing the gospel. Perhaps your family planted other beliefs in you. Perhaps you have beliefs that conflict with what Jesus taught. Please consider which beliefs will lead to a new eternal life with God. It would be helpful to read one of the Gospels of Jesus' life and decide if his teachings are true.

Maybe you are afraid you won't have any pleasure in life anymore. Actually, you will have different pleasures that will be better than your old ones. You will also have some hard times when you follow Jesus, but he will bring you through them.

Maybe you want to make sure in your head before you believe in Jesus. It is good to take time to consider what Jesus says before you decide. But you can't make absolutely sure by logic that it is all true. There is evidence that it is true. But that only brings you to the edge of the chasm; you still have to make a leap of faith. It's normal to have some doubts when you make the leap. Once you leap, God will help your faith grow.

Prayer of belief in the gospel

God, I am willing to make the leap of faith. I believe that Jesus Christ was your divine Son who came to earth and lived a perfect life of love. I believe he died on the cross for my sins, and I receive the forgiveness of sins you are offering me. I believe that Jesus rose from the dead and ascended into heaven, thus conquering sin and death. I believe that you give an eternal life of love with you and your followers in your kingdom to those who repent, believe, and follow.

And Lord, when I say "I believe," I don't just mean that I agree in my mind that these things are true. I mean that I believe in my heart and that I receive these truths and your Son into my spirit. And even though I may have some unbelief, I still believe, and I ask you to help me with my unbelief.

67

Chapter 5—Surrender: Letting Jesus Be Your Leader

The last stage in the process of salvation is surrender. This is not about cleaning up your life before you are saved; rather, it is deciding to start following Jesus and the way he lived life and letting him clean up your life. It means you are asking him to be your boss.

Actually, he will be a much better leader of your life than you are. He is all-powerful and all-knowing, and he loves you more than you love yourself. He leads with kindness and a servant's heart. He will listen to you and values what you think and feel. He created you and knows what is best for your life.

But remember to count the cost before you choose to follow him. Surrender means you are giving your life to him. You are deciding to start following Jesus' way of life. It means challenges and hard times as well as the joy and peace he puts in your heart.

If he is moving in your heart, then don't be afraid to follow him. Take the leap.

Baptism is important because you are declaring that you are dying to your old life and surrendering to God so he can give you new life. It is a physical experience of a spiritual reality.

Remember that you will die eventually, perhaps sooner than later. Then it will be too late to come to Jesus. God will judge your life, and if you choose not to follow him on earth, you will spend eternity away from him. The things you cling to here will pass away when you die. Why cling to them when you can surrender to Jesus and have an eternal new life beginning now?

Prayer to surrender to Jesus and receive salvation

Lord Jesus, I have taken the time to count the cost of following you, and I want to begin to follow. I give up being in charge of my own life. I give up my control of everything, including my hobbies, habits, entertainment, money, sexuality, image, status, career, and especially relationships. I surrender them all to you and accept you as leader over my whole life. Help me to continue to more fully surrender everything to you.

I now fully receive you as my Savior and Lord. Fill me with your Holy Spirit.

Now that I have received the gospel with repentance, belief, and surrender, I thank you for my salvation. Thank you for eternal life. Thank you for adopting me as Your child, bringing me into your kingdom community, and uniting me with you and your followers. Thank you for baptism, in which I will experience this new reality.

Visit Road To New Life Ministries
for growing in the ways of Jesus

On Twitter: @RoadNewLifeMin
On The Web: www.TheRoadToNewLife.com

CHAPTER 7

THE ESSENTIALS OF FOLLOWING JESUS

THIS CHAPTER EXPLAINS the essentials of following Jesus once you are saved. They are the pillars of the daily Christian life.

Who You Are in Christ

When you are saved, God adopts you as his own child, and you have the privileges that come with being a child of God. Now you are in an intimate relationship with the Creator. He is your Father, and he is infinitely better than any earthly father.

You are also a member of God's family. You have brothers and sisters all around the world, and all believers are citizens of God's kingdom. This kingdom community of his love, goodness, and power is all around you, is expanding, and will one day be complete.

You are also free from any condemnation for sin. Jesus took all your condemnation and gave you his righteousness.[1]

You will learn more about your identity in Christ as you read through the New Testament. Remember that this, your core identity, it will give you strength to stand in any situation.

The Pattern of Your Life: Cross and Resurrection

The pattern of the Christian life can be summed up as a life of the cross and resurrection.[2] When we believed, we were crucified with him, and we continue to die to our old selves daily. And when we believed, we rose from the dead with Christ,[3] and we rise daily. One day after Jesus returns, we will completely die to our old life. And one day when he returns, we will completely rise to a new life. So we have already tasted the cross, but it is not yet complete. And we have already tasted resurrection, but it is not yet complete.

Thus, we will have many kinds of victory in our lives, and we can rejoice in such times. And we will have times of suffering, weakness, and loss. But these times only help

---

[1] 2 Corinthians 5:21

[2] See 2 Corinthians 4:10–11; Philippians 3:10–11; 1 Peter 2:21.

[3] Colossians 3:1.

us depend more on God and become more like Christ, who suffered for us.

The Five Channels to Growth

God gives us power and grace through many channels to cleanse us from sin and draw us to himself. In one sense, we are already as close to him as we can be because his Spirit lives in us. But we will spend our entire lives learning to let his Spirit continually transform us to be like Christ. God wants to pour his strength and love into us through various sources. Our role is to live in these channels and receive the life he gives. These various sources of God's grace can be grouped into five types of channels. Each is essential to growth. If one is missing in our lives, it slows us down like a boat trying to sail away with the anchor still dragging in the sand.

1. Living in the Spirit

Galatians 5:16 teaches us that we should "walk by the Spirit, and you will not carry out the desire of the flesh." ("Flesh" is another way of referring to our old natures.) In Romans 8:6 the apostle Paul teaches us that the "mind set on the Spirit is life and peace" and in verse 13 that "by the Spirit you are putting to death the deeds of the body." Ephesians 5:18 tells us to be continuously filled with the Spirit.

Walking by the Spirit keeps us connected to the power and holiness of God. In fact, God's Spirit, our greatest gift in his kingdom, empowers us to live a kingdom life in relationship with God and others. The Holy Spirit is one of the central gifts God promised to believers, and we are unspeakably privileged to have him. Rejoice!

The Spirit is a person and presence in us that can be sensed, and he feels like a life force of love, holiness, and power deep inside us. The Christian life is impossible if we do not have a sense of the Spirit at least some of the time. If you have never sensed the Spirit, then you should find a wise Christian who can help you, perhaps a pastor or a spiritual mentor. Find someone who has experience with walking by the Spirit and ask him or her for guidance.

We can grow in our ability to walk by the Spirit if we continually practice it. Learn to tune your heart and mind to the Spirit within you, draw on his power, and follow his leading.

Walking by the Spirit is both a subjective and objective experience. In our subjective experience, we sometimes have a strong sense of the Spirit, sometimes a weak sense, and sometimes none at all. Objectively, we can learn about walking by the Spirit from Scripture, which is discussed next.

2. Learning from Scripture

The Old and New Testaments are God's words breathed through human beings and set in writing. Hebrews 4:12 states that the "word of God is living and active." Scripture will change us. Second Timothy 3:16 teaches the following:

> All Scripture is inspired by God and is useful to teach us what is true and to make us realize what is wrong in our lives. It correct us when we are wrong and teaches us to do what is right. God uses it to prepare and equip his people to do every good work. (NLT)

The New Testament is the collection of the life and teachings of Jesus and his apostles. They reveal all the important spiritual truths for following God. When we read and meditate on the Scriptures, the Holy Spirit uses the words to reveal truth to our hearts and to draw us near to God in faith and love. Scripture will convict our hearts and guide us to repent of sin. It will help burn away the impurities that keep us from receiving the true life God wants for us. And Scripture is like fuel for our spiritual fire. Without it our fire dies out.

We should not come to Scripture just to gain knowledge. Its purpose is to build a relationship with God and others. We can easily get caught in the trap of thinking that if we become knowledgeable about Scripture, then we will become spiritual. But that attitude only leads to

> *Scripture is like fuel for our spiritual fire.*

having a relationship with a book, not a person. We should come to Scripture with open hearts, asking the Spirit to lead us into knowing God and ourselves.

3. Fellowship

Scripture is clear about our need for a relationship with other believers to grow spiritually. And other believers need us too. We need to share love,[4] comfort, encouragement, burdens, confession of sin,[5] teaching, prayer, guidance, and the Lord's Supper.

Pride can tempt us to live the Christian life on our own. The Enemy knows that if he can get us isolated, then he has a much better chance of torpedoing us with sin. He knows that without help, we will not have the strength to overcome trials and defeat sin.

But if we have relationships with other believers and if we open up our lives to them and ask for help and prayer to overcome our difficulties, then the Enemy cannot win.

---

[4] See Colossians 3:12–16 for how believers should treat each other.
[5] James 5:16.

One person alone may not be able to climb over a ten-foot wall, but with a rope and a team working together, the whole team can make it over a wall.

Most importantly, God desires us to love one another. In fact, the apostle John said that "if someone says 'I love God,' and hates his brother, he is a liar; for the one who does not love his brother whom he has seen, cannot love God whom he has not seen."[6] Jesus said that the world will know we are followers of Jesus by the way we love one another.[7] Learning to love other believers, even the difficult ones, is our main goal in fellowship.

Church attendance is not necessarily fellowship. In most churches believers don't spend time on Sunday morning sharing their lives with one another and encouraging and praying for one another. This usually happens in a small group, whether formal or informal. We cannot afford to let Sunday morning trick us into thinking we have fellowship when we really don't. Sunday morning is good for receiving teaching and for worship, both of which are important. But there is more to fellowship.

4. Prayer

The great Christian teachers over the centuries considered prayer the most essential activity of the Christian life. Prayer is simply the act of relating to or communicating with God. Without prayer there is no relationship with God, just as in a

> *Without prayer there is no relationship with God, just as in a marriage there is no relationship without communication.*

[6] 1 John 4:20.
[7] John 13:35.

marriage there is no relationship without communication. And relationship with God is the whole purpose of growth; in fact, it is the definition of growth. How can you know your spouse if you never talk with him or her? How can you know God if you don't talk with him? How can we love God with all our hearts if we say only a few sentences to him every day? Could a marriage survive on that? If our "marriage" with God is important to us, we should be able to set aside ten to fifteen minutes a day to pray.

There are many types of prayer, just as there are many ways to communicate. Spend time studying the Lord's Prayer in Matthew 6:9–13. We can make requests, we can give thanks, we can praise God, we can admit our weaknesses and failures, we can confess our temptations, we can ask for forgiveness, we can ask questions, we can ask for help, we can express our anger or fear or pain, we can sing, we can cry, we can reflect on his Scripture, and we can just silently be with him.

Prayer is not just a one-way street. God also wants to communicate with us, so we should listen for his voice. Sometimes he speaks by giving us an impression or a confidence about something or an insight or a Scripture, or a quiet voice we can hear in our hearts. His voice comes with peace and love—even when his words bother us.

Since God is our Father, he wants to hear what we have to say, and he wants to listen to what we think and feel. He already knows what's in our hearts, but it makes all the difference when we take the time to express it—just as an earthly father may know how his child is feeling, but he still wants to hear him say it. By saying what he feels, the child shows that he trusts his father with his heart. This opens up the mutual flow of love between their two hearts.

Expressing ourselves to God opens our hearts to the flow of love that is always coming from his heart. Then his love flows from our hearts back into his heart and into the hearts of those around us.

5. Loving Others

Loving our neighbors is both a cause and effect of growth. Look for neighbors, coworkers, and strangers to show kindness to. As we love others, we will find God's love capturing our hearts. When we exercise the measure of love he has already given us, even when we don't like it, then his love grows in us. Thus, loving others becomes a channel of spiritual growth.

This is especially true about loving those who hurt us. Jesus did not teach us just to love other believers and those who are good to us. He pointed out, "If you are kind only to your friends, how are you different from anyone else? Even pagans do that" (Matt. 5:47 NLT). So a Christian is someone who loves others unconditionally.

Loving those who are hard to love breaks down old, hardened areas of our hearts that resist the law of love. And when we fail, it forces us to depend more on God. It is all a process of repenting from our old, sinful, unloving ways and placing our will inside his will. This surrender allows him to make us more like Christ. Then, as transformed citizens of the kingdom of God, his light can shine even more brightly through us to the world.

Your Future

Another essential principle of following Jesus is learning to live with a heavenly perspective. This means living our lives, knowing that we are citizens of heaven[8] and will spend eternity in the kingdom of heaven. Jesus said, "Don't

---

[8] Philippians 3:20.

store up treasures here on earth . . . Store your treasures in heaven."[9] Colossians 3:2 states, "Set your minds on things above, not on earthly things" (NIV). Our future is heaven.

Since we are his children, he is waiting to give us an immense inheritance. Our inheritance from him is his kingdom, and he gives some of it now and the rest in the next life. In this life we receive his Spirit, his love, and his power in our hearts, but we still have to struggle in a sinful world, and we are far from perfect. In the next life he will give us the rest of his kingdom.[10] He will remove all sin from our new world and remove all sin from us. We will have no more pain and no more tears.[11] We will live in complete joy and harmony with God and his followers in a never-ending community of love. God will give us his own glory so that we "will shine like the sun in the kingdom of [our] Father." [12]

God is going to give us rewards in heaven. Jesus said, "Love your enemies! Do good to them . . . Then your reward from heaven will be very great."[13] He also told us to rejoice when we are rejected for Christ's sake because we will have great reward in heaven.[14] At the end of the last book of the Bible, the

> *You will be rewarded with treasures in heaven for the ways you loved God and loved others in this life.*

book of Revelation, Jesus said, "I am coming soon, and my

---

[9] Matthew 6:19–20 NLT.

[10] See Revelation 21–22.

[11] Revelation 21:4.

[12] Matthew 13:43 NIV.

[13] Luke 6:35 NLT.

[14] Luke 6:22–23.

reward is with me, to repay all according to their deeds."[15] God will give us rewards for our good works. Who can doubt that a reward from God in heaven is worth more than all the wealth on earth?

Let us meditate on and absorb this eternal reality so that it immunizes us against our love for earthly wealth and status. As we begin to actually believe the truth about our future, we will find ourselves freer of worldly strivings and more motivated to store up treasure in heaven.

You *will* be rewarded with treasures in heaven for the ways you loved God and others in this life. As you believe this, you will develop a heavenly perspective about this life and learn to live in that spiritual reality. God's kingdom is "not of this world."[16] If you try to live by the world's priorities, then you will enter the next life with regret. You will miss out on the great rewards God wanted to give you.

It is extremely important to believe what God says about the spiritual reality we live in. Jesus Christ is above all the rulers and powers we see around us,[17] and "in Him all things hold together."[18]

God is everywhere, working in people's hearts and bringing history to its great conclusion according to his will. He wants you to be part of this.

Visit Road To New Life Ministries
for growing in the ways of Jesus

On Twitter: @RoadNewLifeMin
On The Web: www.TheRoadToNewLife.com

---

[15] Revelation 22:12 NLT.

[16] John 18:36.

[17] Ephesians 1:21–22.

[18] Colossians 1:17.

APPENDIX

THE PROBLEM OF THE NO-COST GOSPEL

> The world does not want to eliminate Christianity, it is not that straightforward, nor does it have that much character. No, it wants it proclaimed falsely, using eternity to give a flavor to the enjoyment of life.[1]
>
> —Soren Kierkegaard

HOPEFULLY, YOU WILL have opportunities to share the gospel with others. When the time comes, we need to be careful how we share it. Do we proclaim the gospel of salvation in such a way that it truly transforms people? Or do the majority of the people who respond to our salvation invitations never display converted hearts? The culprit may be a "no-cost" gospel. This is a gospel that minimizes the more challenging elements of the gospel of salvation.

---

[1] Charles E. Moore, ed., *Provocations: Spiritual Writings of Kierkegaard* (Farmington, PA: Plough Publishing, 2002), 4–5.

81

The most common problems with salvation invitations are related to (1) conviction of sin, (2) repentance, (3) surrender, and (4) counting the cost. These topics are minimized or omitted in most salvation invitations. This no-cost gospel is damaging the health of the church. Researcher George Barna found, "A majority of the people who made a first-time 'decision' for Christ were no longer connected to a Christian church within just eight weeks of having made such a decision!"[2]

How often do speakers frame their messages in such a way as to produce actual conviction and remorse for sin? How often are listeners encouraged to take some time to consider whether they truly want to leave behind their old lives and become followers of Jesus? Surely the most important decision of a person's life merits such reflection.

If our listeners are never challenged in this way, how can we expect true conversion? Will the Holy Spirit work if we don't speak all the words of the gospel? Speaking the right words is truly up to us, as the apostle Paul said. "How will they believe in Him whom they have not heard?" (Rom. 10:14)

Listeners today need much more explanation of the gospel than they usually receive. The Jews to whom Jesus and his apostles preached already knew from Scripture that their sin separated them from God, that they needed forgiveness, and that they needed to repent and make God their Lord. But most people are taught just the opposite—that they are basically good, that their occasional "mistakes" are not so serious, and that they are lord over their own lives. Our salvation invitations need to dispel these misconceptions.

If there is any teaching, any message, that must be explained carefully and fully, it is the gospel. It is the foundation of the church and of a Christian's life. If the foundation is weak, the building will not stand up to the storms of the world. I hope this book can be used to overcome this problem.

[2] George Barna, *Second Coming of the Church* (Nashville: Word, 1998), 2.

Some of the following material has already been covered in this book, but it is helpful to repeat.

The State of Evangelism in America Today

The most common type of salvation invitation heard today usually begins with a short discussion of what Jesus can do for the listeners' lives, then perhaps a brief explanation that Jesus died for them so they can be forgiven. Then listeners are invited to say a prayer something like this: "Jesus, I believe that you are the Son of God and that you died for my sins. Please come in to my life and forgive my sins. I accept you as my Lord and Savior. I accept your gift of eternal life and thank you that I am going to heaven." The entire presentation of the actual gospel and the prayer often lasts less than five minutes.

Such a prayer often does not produce true conversion. They said they were sinners, but there wasn't time for conviction of sin. Moreover, they did not repent of their sins. Even if the words "I repent" had been added, it is unlikely that there would have been time for true repentance to form. The idea of lordship was only introduced in the prayer, so they have not had time to count the cost ahead of time. Perhaps the Holy Spirit will complete the process, but normally the Spirit depends on the speaker to speak the words. Those who pray such prayers often go away unchanged but hoping they are going to heaven. Often the speaker tells them they are saved now, but this is a false assurance.

I believe the spread of this kind of no-cost gospel goes a long way toward explaining the surveys conducted by George Barna and others that reveal the great lack of transformation in American Christians. Sixty-five percent of American adults claim they have made a personal commitment to Jesus Christ that is important in their lives today.[3] But sadly, only 13 percent of American adults use the Bible as the source for their moral and ethical decision making.[4] Nominalism is a big problem in the church today.

The Elements of the Gospel

The presentation of the gospel[5] may be divided into five elements:
(1) God loves us, but our sin separates us from him,
(2) Jesus is the Son of God who died for our sins,
(3) we need to repent of our sins,
(4) we need to believe and receive Jesus and his forgiveness of our sins, and
(5) we need make an initial surrender to Jesus Christ as Lord of our life.

More briefly: (1) sin, (2) Christ, (3) repentance, (4) belief, and (5) surrender. As mentioned earlier in the book, we can more easily remember these five elements when giving salvation invitations by forming an acronym from them. By adding a *u* after the third element, we arrive at the acronym SCRuBS (as in "Jesus scrubs us clean").

Most salvation invitations focus only on elements (2) and (4). But it is the other three that are the "cost" of the

---

[3] George Barna, *The State of the Church 2002* (Ventura, CA: Issachar Resources, 2002), 62.

[4] Barna Research Group, http://www.barna.org/barna-update/article/5-barna-update/67-americans-are-most-likely-to-base-truth-on-feelings, Barna Update February 12, 2002.

[5] Strictly speaking, the gospel or *euangelion* is the key facts regarding Jesus' life. See *International Standard Bible Encyclopedia*, ed. Geoffrey W. Bromiley, "Gospel" (Grand Rapids: Eerdmans, 1986), 532. These facts are the following : he was the Messiah prophesied in the Old Testament, he died for our sins, and God his Father resurrected him from the dead (see 1 Cor. 15:1–7). For convenience, in this appendix I use the word *gospel* to include both the gospel and the responses to the gospel God expects.

gospel, and if they are not prominent in our presentations, then we are robbing the listener of the full power of the gospel to save and transform him or her.[6]

Conviction of sin

Conviction of sin is the necessary foundation for repentance as well as for the entire salvation invitation. Scripture states that "all have sinned and fall short of the glory of God" (Rom. 3:23) and "the wages of sin is death" (Rom. 6:23). Great leaders of the church have acknowledged this need for conviction of sin. Charles Finney stated, "It is of great importance that the sinner should be made to feel his guilt."[7] Philip Melanchthon, chief theologian to Martin Luther, taught "The beginning of repentance consists of that work of the Law by which the Spirit of God terrifies and confounds consciences."[8]

Until a listener knows he or she has sinned against God and thus will be eternally separated from him, he or she has little to be saved from. Thus, invitations to groups should address common sins of the flesh as well as common sins of the heart in order to break open listeners' hearts. For example, speakers can discuss dishonesty, immorality, unforgiveness, meanness, rebellion, pride, gossip, strife, rejection of God, selfishness, vengefulness, and materialism to convict listeners of their sin. When speaking one-on-one, we can judge what is appropriate for that listener. We should always remember to be kind, not judgmental. And

---

[6] At the beginning of this appendix, I listed "counting the cost" as a separate problem of salvation invitations. Since it applies to each of these three elements, it will not be treated separately.

[7] Ray Comfort, *Hell's Best Kept Secret* (Springdale, PA: Whitaker House, 1989), 24.

[8] Ibid., 50.

we should remember to begin with God's love as shown in chapter 1 of this book.

Repentance

In the New Testament, *repentance* (from the Greek *metanoia*) is "a turning away from evil and a turning to God."[9] Bauer, Arndt, and Gingrich's *Greek-English Lexicon of the New Testament* defines *metanoia* as "a change of mind," "turning about," and "conversion."[10] The *International Standard Bible Encyclopedia* states, "Change of mind is the dominant idea of [repentance], while the accompanying grief and reform of life are necessary consequences."[11]

Repentance is not simply sorrow or regret. It is the decision of the heart and mind to turn away from the old lifestyle, the old path. Jesus requires this initial breaking of self before we enter his kingdom. Listeners need to be challenged to turn away from their materialism, dishonesty, immorality, meanness, self-sufficiency, and self-lordship.

Jesus included repentance in the Great Commission he issued to his followers: "[I]t is written, that the Christ would suffer and rise again from the dead the third day, and that repentance for forgiveness of sins would be proclaimed in His name to all the nations" (Luke 24:46–47).

Repentance was equally important in the apostles' preaching for salvation. At the conclusion of the first evangelistic sermon, Peter called his listeners to repent: "Now when they heard this, they were pierced to the heart,

---

[9] *Theological Dictionary of the New Testament*, ed. Kittel, "*metanoia*" discussed in article on "*nous*," (Grand Rapids: Eerdmans, 1967).

[10] Walter Bauer and others, *Greek-English Lexicon of the New Testament*, "metanoia," (Chicago: University of Chicago Press, 1979), 512.

[11] *International Standard Bible Encyclopedia*, ed. Geoffrey W. Bromiley, "Repent" (Grand Rapids: Eerdmans, 1986), 136.

and said to Peter and the rest of the apostles, 'Brethren, what shall we do?' Peter said to them, 'Repent, and each of you be baptized in the name of Jesus Christ for the forgiveness of your sins; and you will receive the gift of the Holy Spirit' (Acts 2:37–38).[12]

Paul summed up his teaching thus: "I have declared to both Jews and Greeks that they must turn to God in repentance and have faith in our Lord Jesus" (Acts 20:21 NIV).[13]

Hence Scripture makes it clear that there is no forgiveness of sins without repentance. Thus, instead of downplaying repentance in our salvation invitations, we need to be especially intentional about convicting our listeners of sin and challenging them to repentance. Otherwise, we risk giving them a false assurance of salvation.

Theologian Thomas Oden explains:

> To make the call to repentance and faith plausible is the perennial task of Christian preaching. When it is neglected, every other aspect of the mission of the church stands imperiled. Preaching that lacks the courage to call hearers to repent is limp and timid.[14]

Invitations should *teach* listeners what it means to repent. It does not mean that the listener needs to stop sinning—that would be impossible. Repentance is not turning one's life around; it is merely the decision to turn around. God turns one's life around through Christ when we make the decision. He is just waiting for the listener to agree with him about his condition and his need.

---

[12] See also Acts 3:19.

[13] See also Acts 17:30.

[14] Thomas C. Oden, *Life in the Spirit, Systematic Theology: vol. 3* (Peabody, MA: Prince Press, 2001, reprinted from 1992 HarperSanFrancisco edition), 79.

Surrender

Surrender is the decision to let Jesus be one's leader or Lord. I do not mean that one has to actually be following Jesus as Lord in order to be saved; rather, one has to make an initial decision to follow him. Surrender is turning to God in Christ so he can make us like Christ and produce good works in us through his Spirit. This decision is the one that actually establishes the believer into an ongoing relationship with Jesus.

Jesus and his apostles made it clear that surrender is required for salvation. In Luke 14:26–28 Jesus explains what is required of a disciple[15]: "If you want to be my follower you must love me more than your own father and mother, wife and children, brothers and sisters—yes, more than your own life. Otherwise, you cannot be my disciple [*mathetes*]. And you cannot be my disciple if you do not carry your own cross and follow me. But don't begin until you count the cost" (NLT).

Paul states: "For if you confess with your mouth that Jesus is Lord and believe in your heart that God raised him from the dead, you will be saved" (Rom. 10:9–10 NLT).

This confession of lordship is not simply mental assent.[16] It is a declaration of personal submission. Hence, we should not shy away from fully challenging listeners in our salvation invitations to surrender their lives to Jesus. Respected teacher John Stott states: ". . . in issuing the

---

[15] In the Gospels Jesus uses the word *disciple* (*mathetes in Greek*) to describe all those who followed him, i.e., to all the believers. A *mathetes* in Jesus' time was an apprentice or pupil. In the Gospels it does not refer to a higher class of Christian; rather "Christian" and "disciple" are synonymous. This is seen in Acts 11:26 where it states that the "disciples were first called Christians in Antioch." Thus, Jesus' words regarding disciples apply to all Christians.

[16] See James 2:19.

gospel invitation we have no liberty to conceal the cost of discipleship."[17] Some have a fear that emphasizing surrender may unnecessarily turn away seekers, but we are not doing them a favor by downplaying it; instead, we may be robbing them of true conversion. A prepared heart should welcome surrender; the person is getting free from the burden of running his or her own life.

Well-known author A. W. Tozer stated, "But how can we insist and teach that our Lord Jesus Christ can be our Savior without being our Lord? How can we continue to teach that we can be saved without any thought of obedience to our Sovereign Lord?"[18] "Under the working of the Spirit of God through such men as Finney and Wesley, no one would ever dare to rise in a meeting and say, 'I am a Christian' if he had not surrendered his whole being to God and had taken Jesus Christ as his Lord. It was only then that he could say, 'I am saved!'"[19]

Conclusion

The no-cost gospel hurts listeners. Many who respond are left in a "partial-birth" state, which frustrates both themselves and those who try to minister to them. Thus, it sabotages the mission of the church to make disciples of Jesus.

Preaching the whole gospel may or may not result in fewer "decisions," but we will be fulfilling our mission to make disciples—which is our calling and joy. The gospel is

[17] Published by the Lausanne Committee for World Evangelization from Lausanne Occasional Paper 3, section 4.C. Go to: http://www.lausanne. org/all-documents/lop-3.html. The paper is a commentary by John Stott on the Lausanne Covenant of 1974.

[18] A.W. Tozer, *I Call It Heresy* (Camp Hill, PA: Christian Publications, 1991), 7.

[19] Ibid., 13.

the best news the world has ever known. It is freedom from attempts at salvation through our own efforts. If we love the people Christ died for, then we will not neutralize its power.

When we give our salvation invitations, we should remember conviction of sin, repentance, and surrender. Give the words time to sink in so the hearers can count the cost. Perhaps we can give listeners a copy of one of the Gospels before they decide.

We might be surprised at what happens if we believe in the power of the whole gospel. As Paul said, "I am not ashamed of this Good News about Christ. It is the power of God at work, saving everyone who believes" (Rom. 1:16 NLT).

ADDITIONAL HELPFUL READING

Gordon D. Fee and Douglas Stuart, *How to Read the Bible Book by Book: A Guided Tour* (Grand Rapids, MI: Zondervan, 2002).

This outstanding guide to reading the Bible was written by top Bible scholars. It provides a summary of each book along with the key concepts and themes for that book. The authors also help the reader understand how each book fits into the larger context of the Bible. An invaluable tool.

C. S. Lewis, *Mere Christianity* (San Francisco: HarperOne, 2001).

This book is one of the great classics on what Christianity is all about. It combines careful reasoning and spiritual insight. It is highly recommended for anyone wanting to understand and think through the Christian faith more carefully.

Brennan Manning, *The Ragamuffin Gospel: Good News for the Bedraggled, Beat-Up, and Burnt Out* (Portland, OR: Multnomah Books, 2005).

The author is a former priest who fell into alcoholism. He helps readers understand God's great unconditional love for them and how he wants to be their intimate Father. God loves you just as you are and wants to give you his blessings. A very popular book.

N. T. Wright, *Simply Christian: Why Christianity Makes Sense* (San Francisco: HarperSanFrancisco, 2006).

This excellent explanation of the Christian faith in plain language is by one of the greatest New Testament scholars in the world. Wright answers the questions many people often have about Christianity. He looks at the issues of justice, beauty, relationships, pain, and hope and explains how they point to Jesus. A highly regarded book.

http://www.BibleGateway.com

This Web site lets you read the Bible or look up specific verses in many different versions and languages. It also offers other helpful resources, including a topical index to the Bible.

Visit www.TheRoadToNewLife.com.

DISCIPLE

PUBLISHING